Mysterious

Arya Bàhram

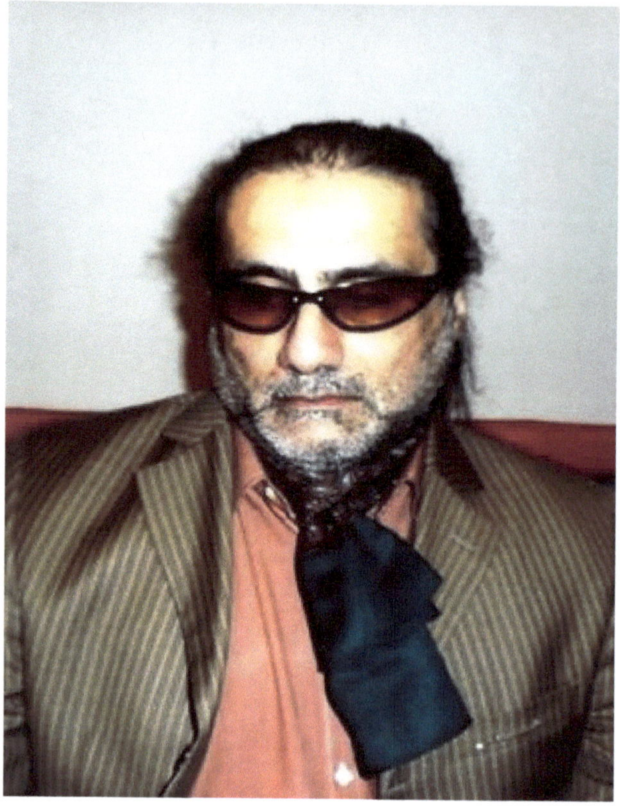

Mysterious

Arya Bàhram

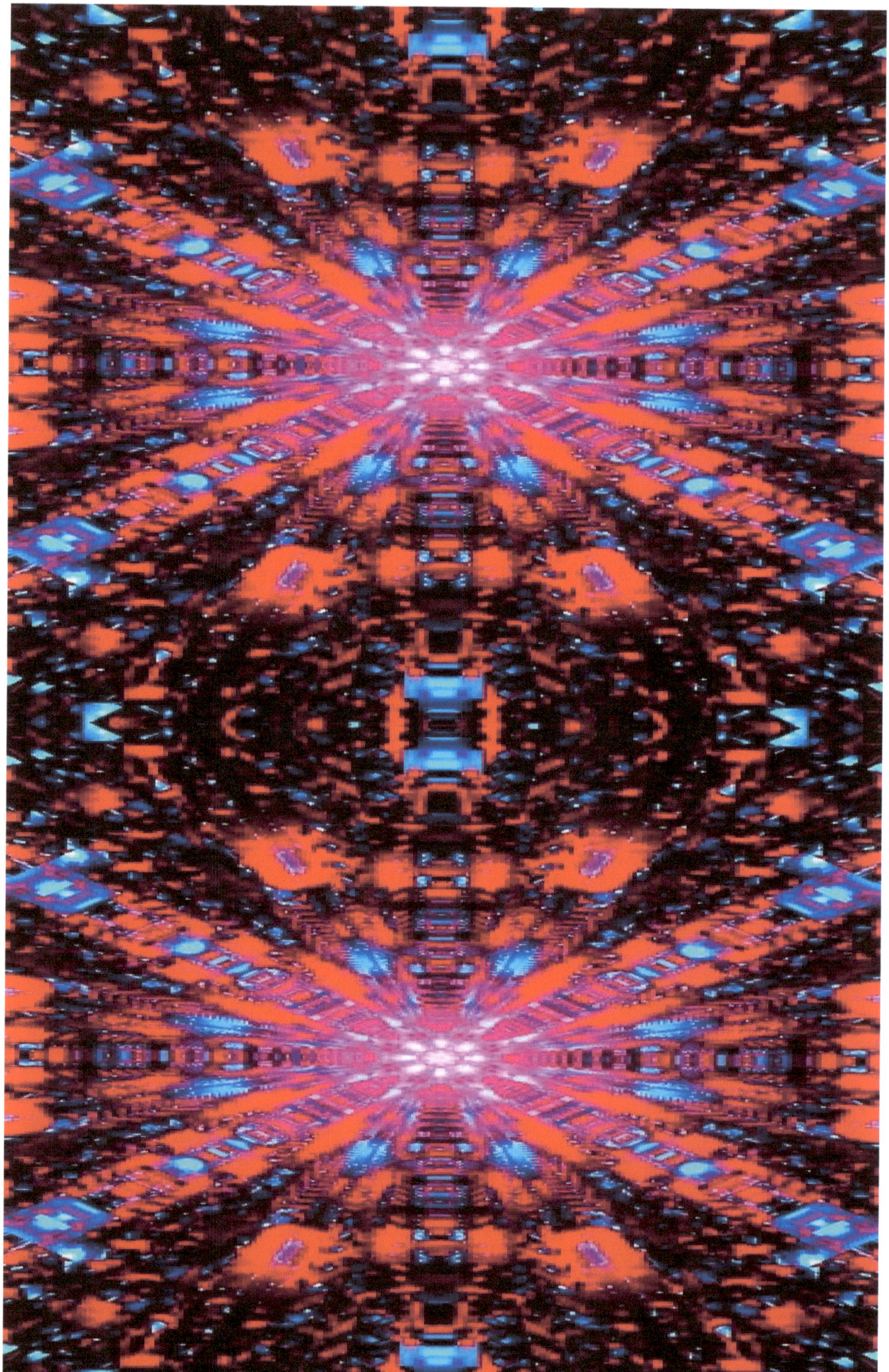

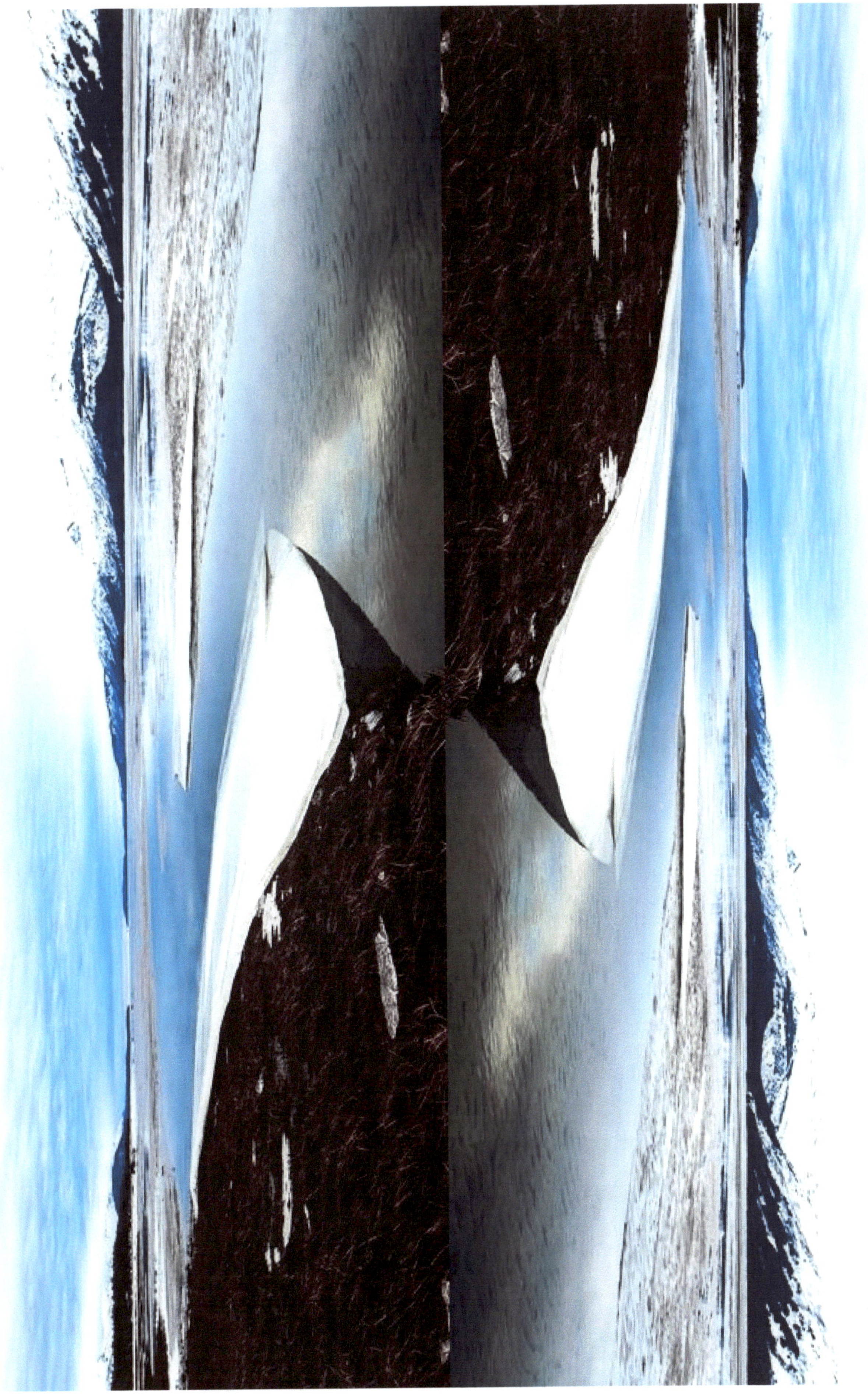

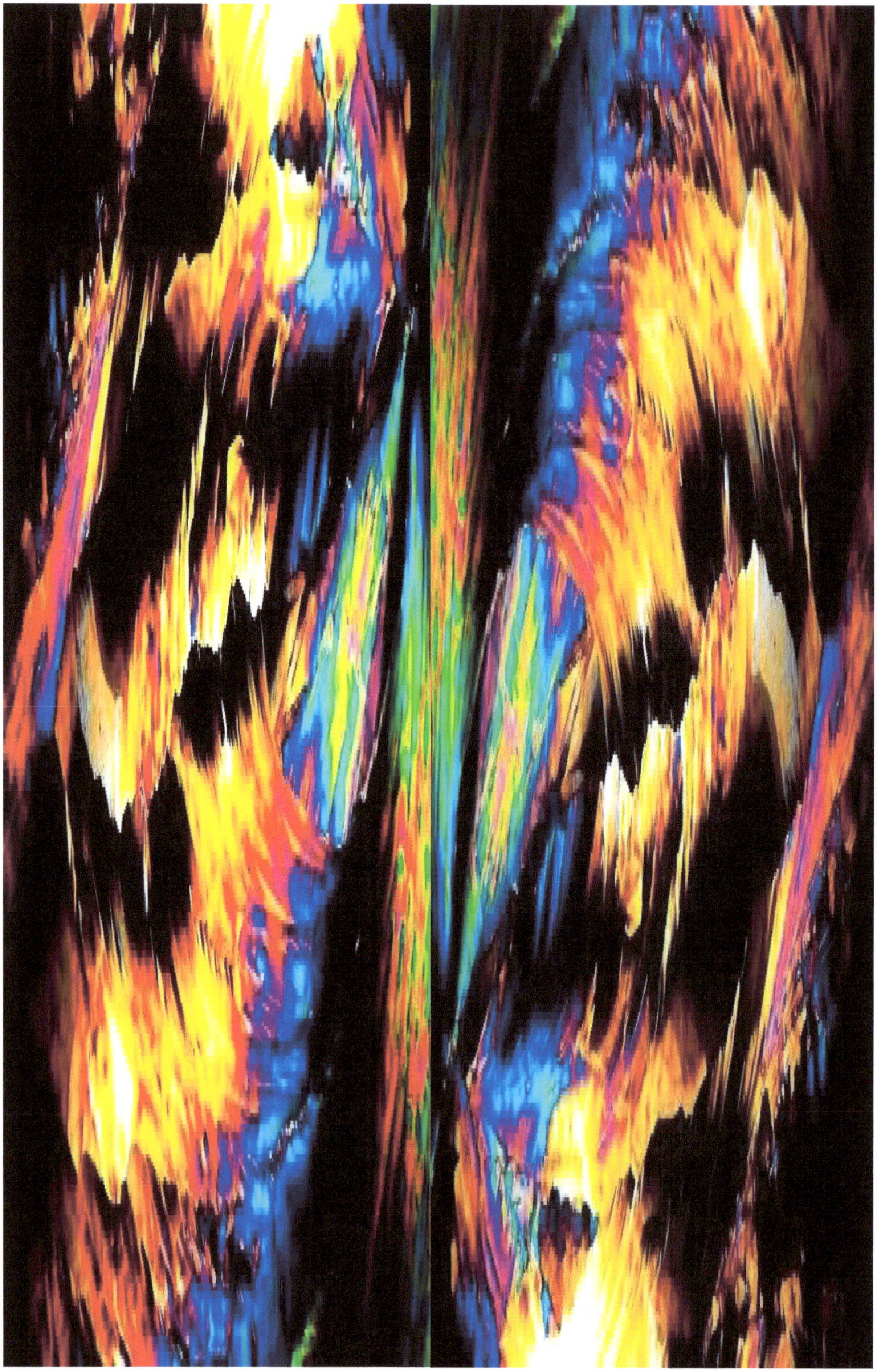

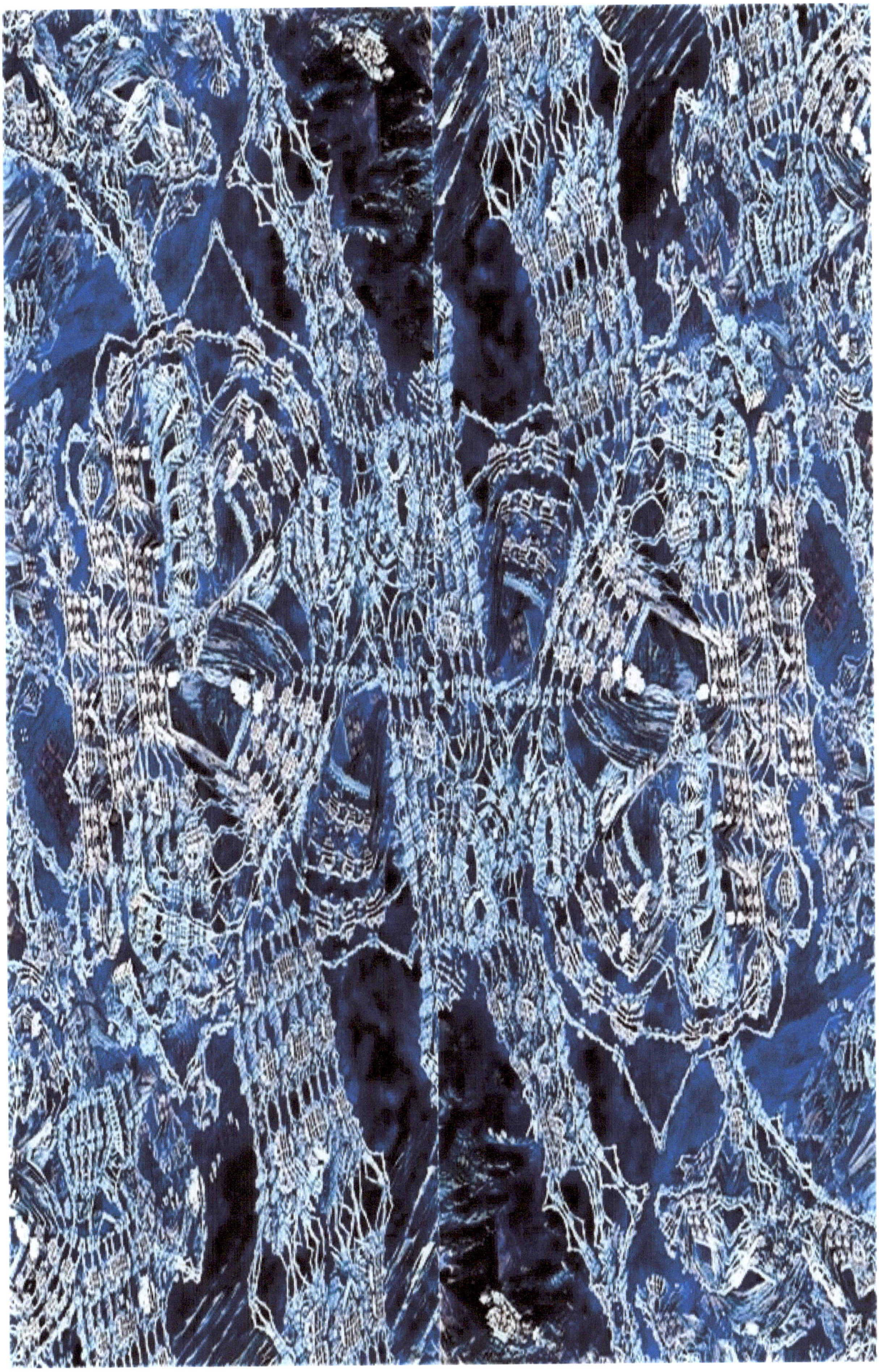

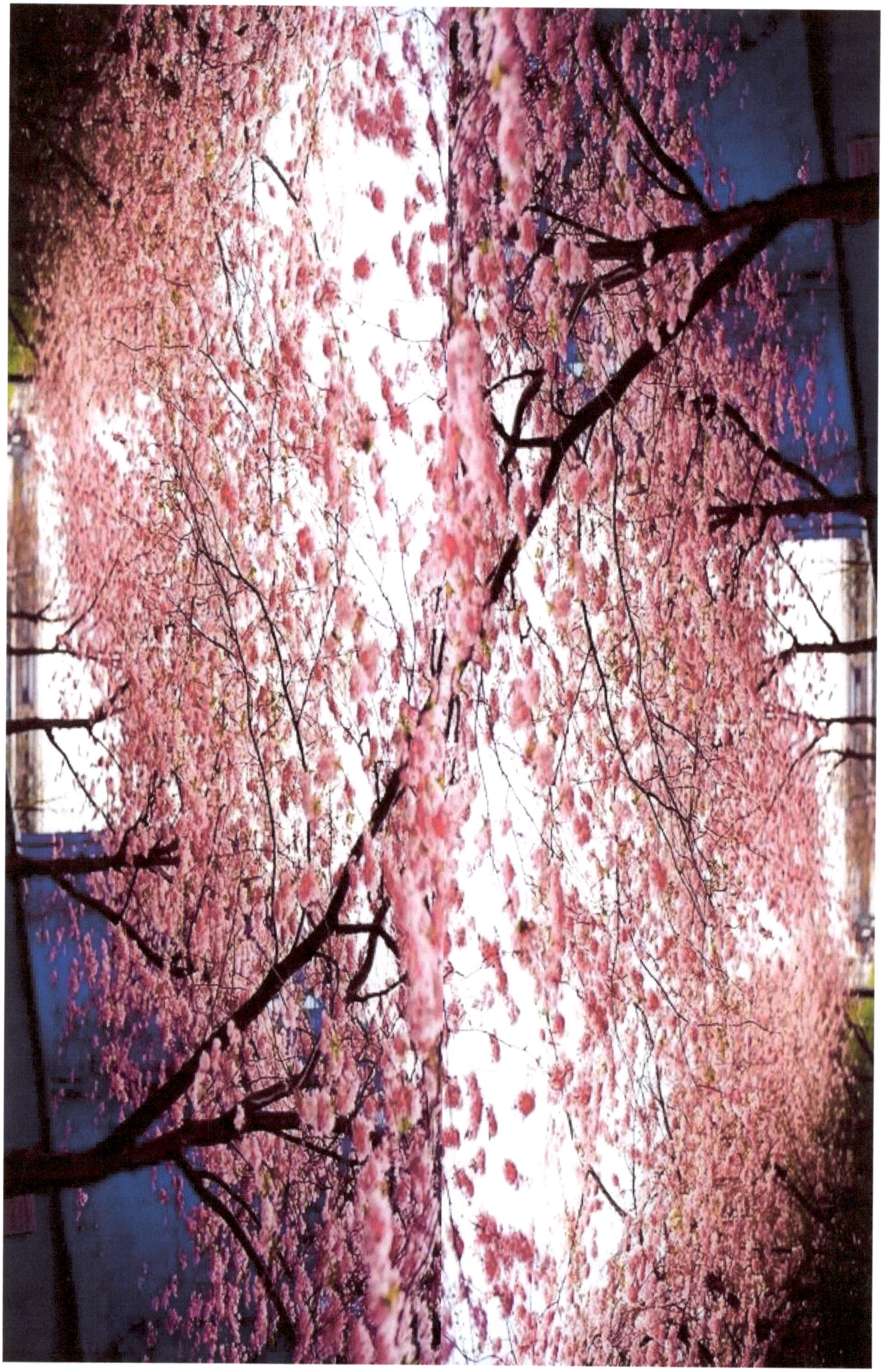

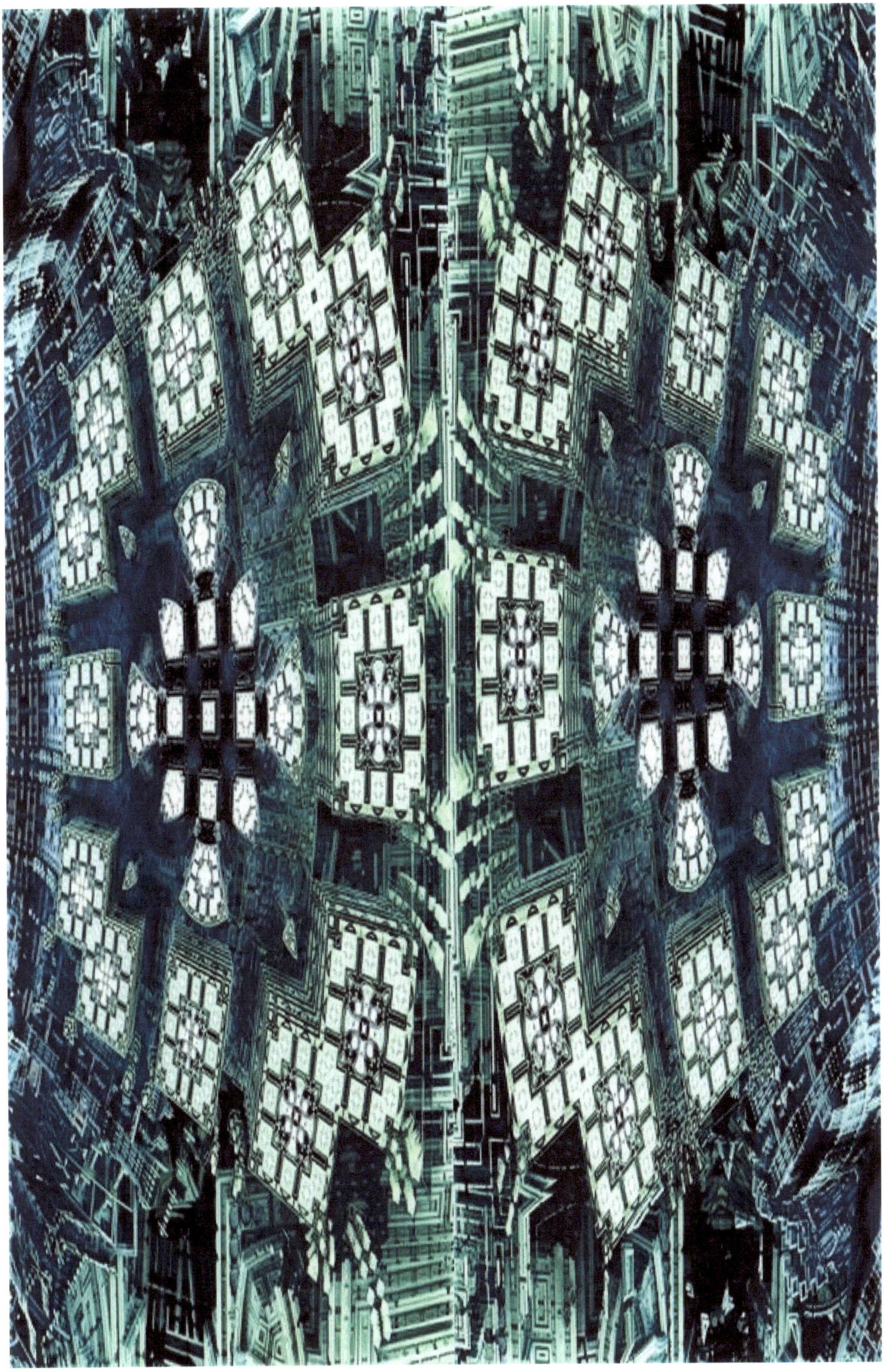

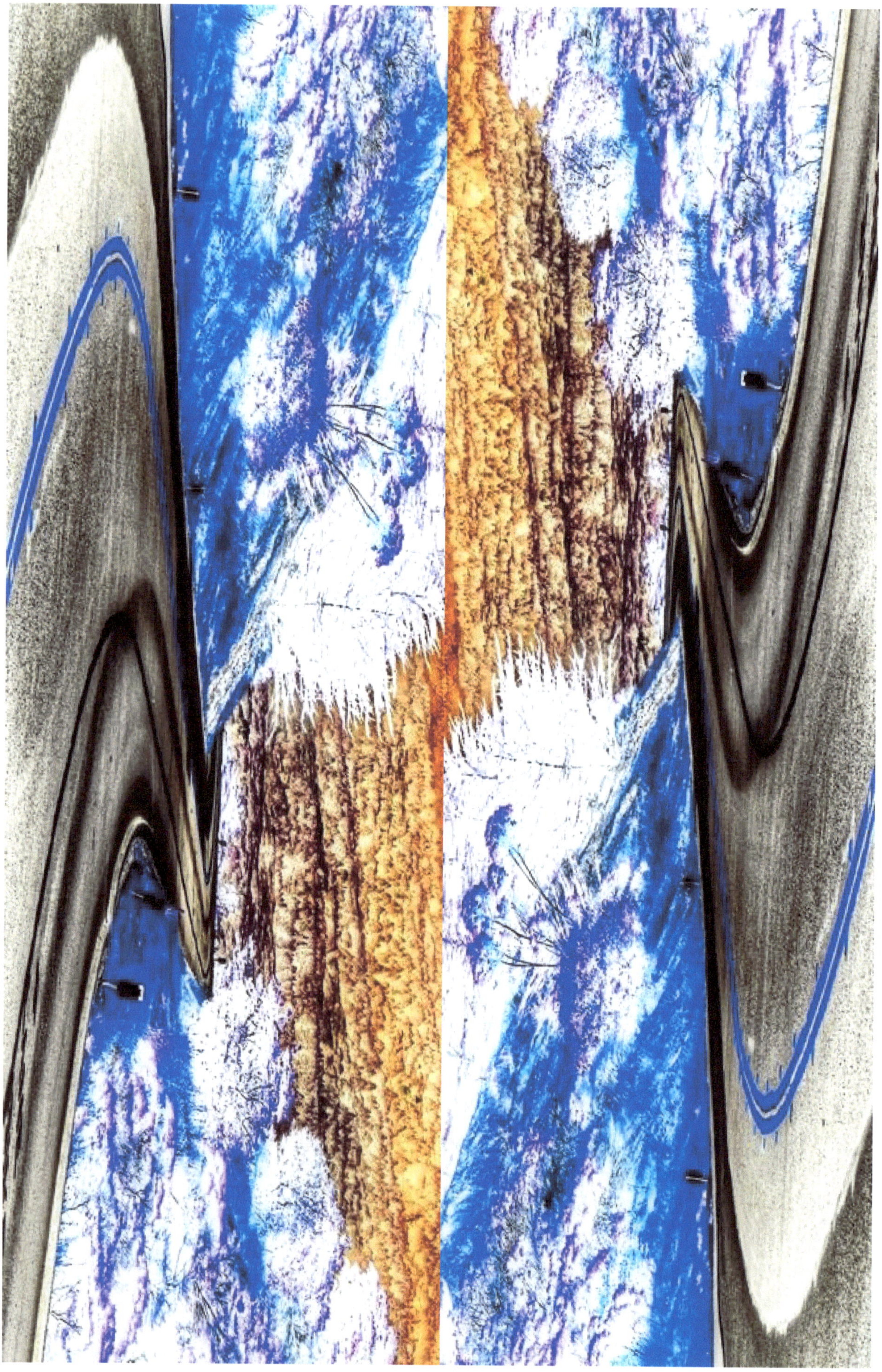

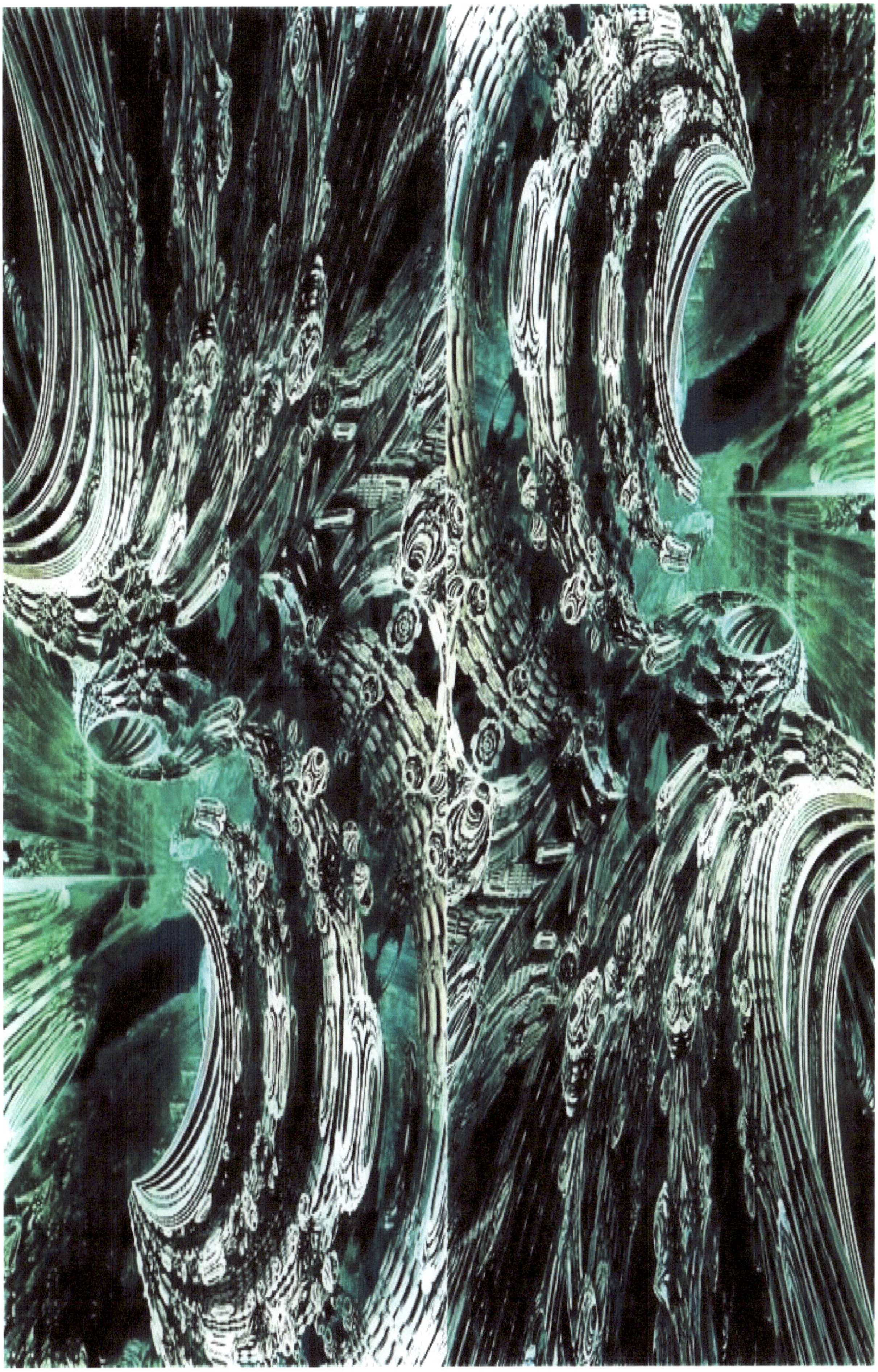

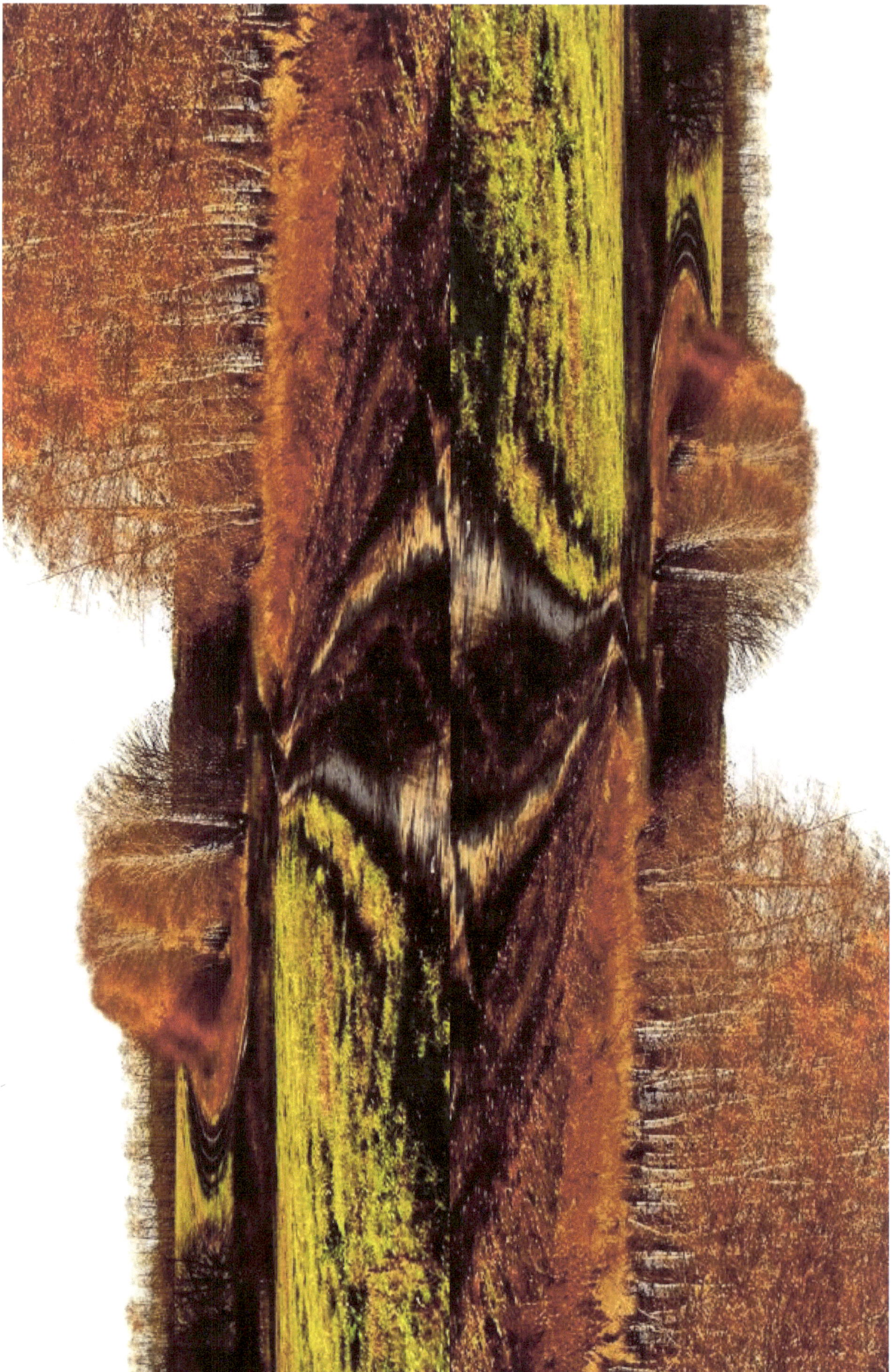

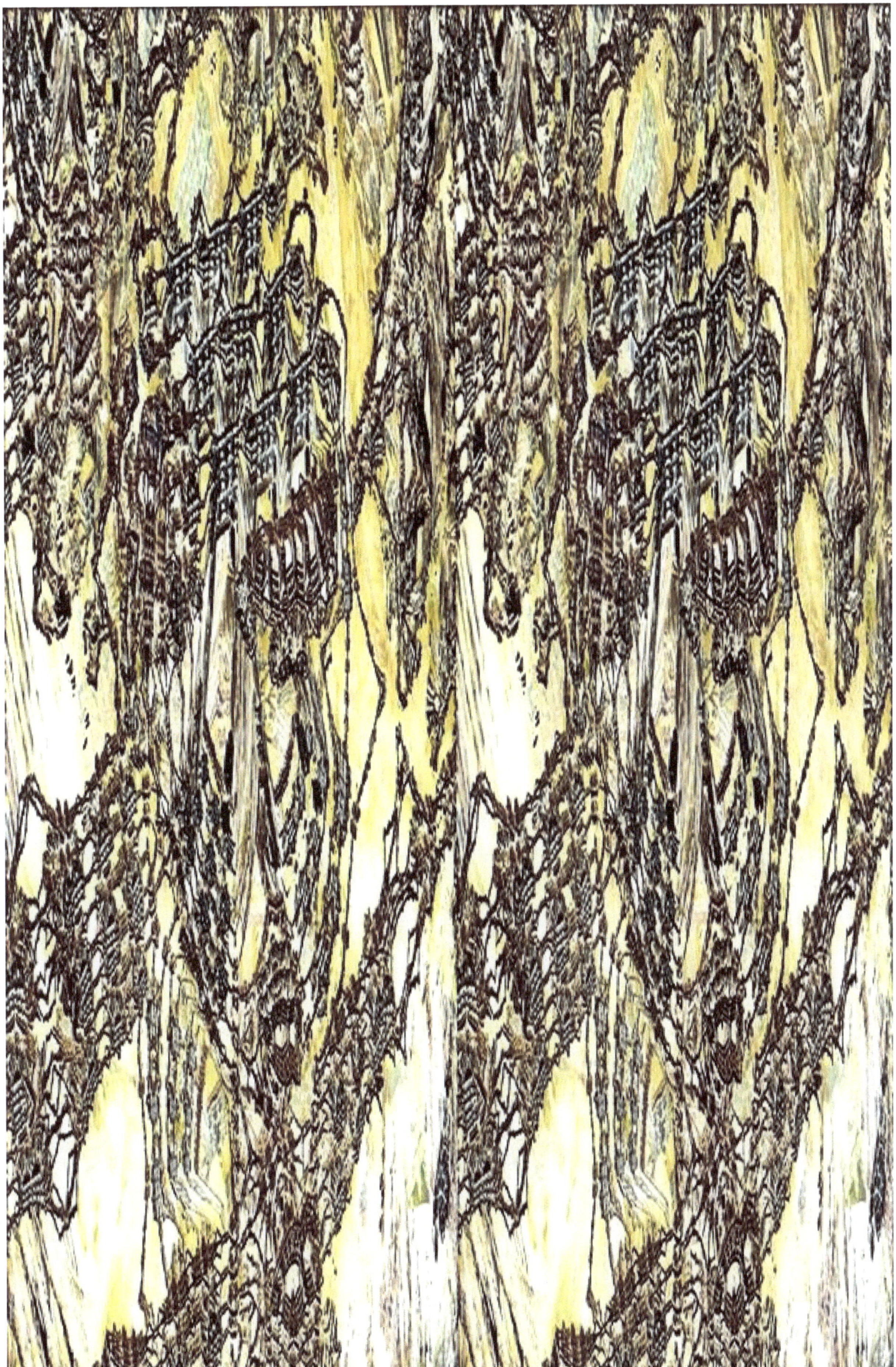

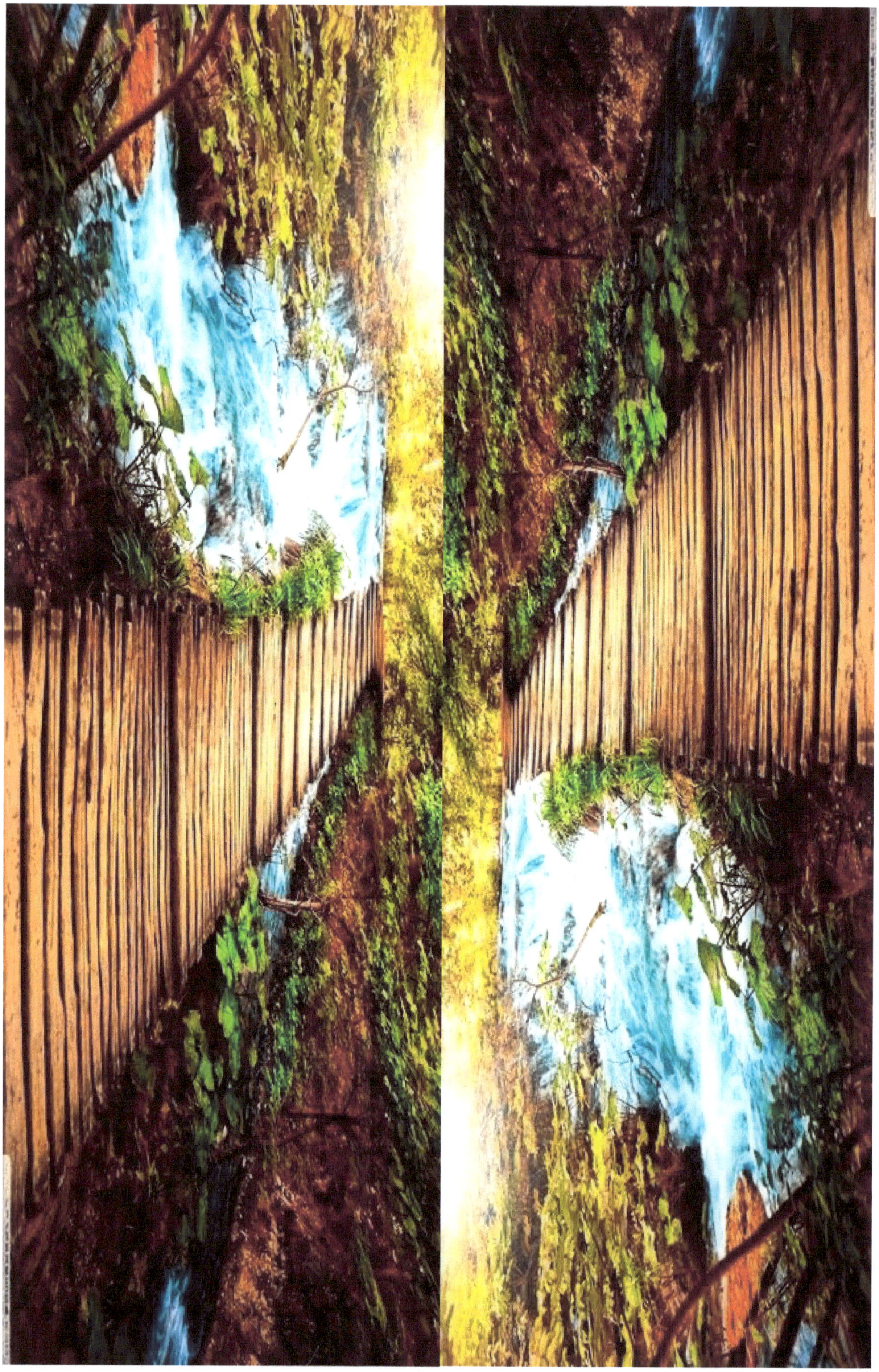

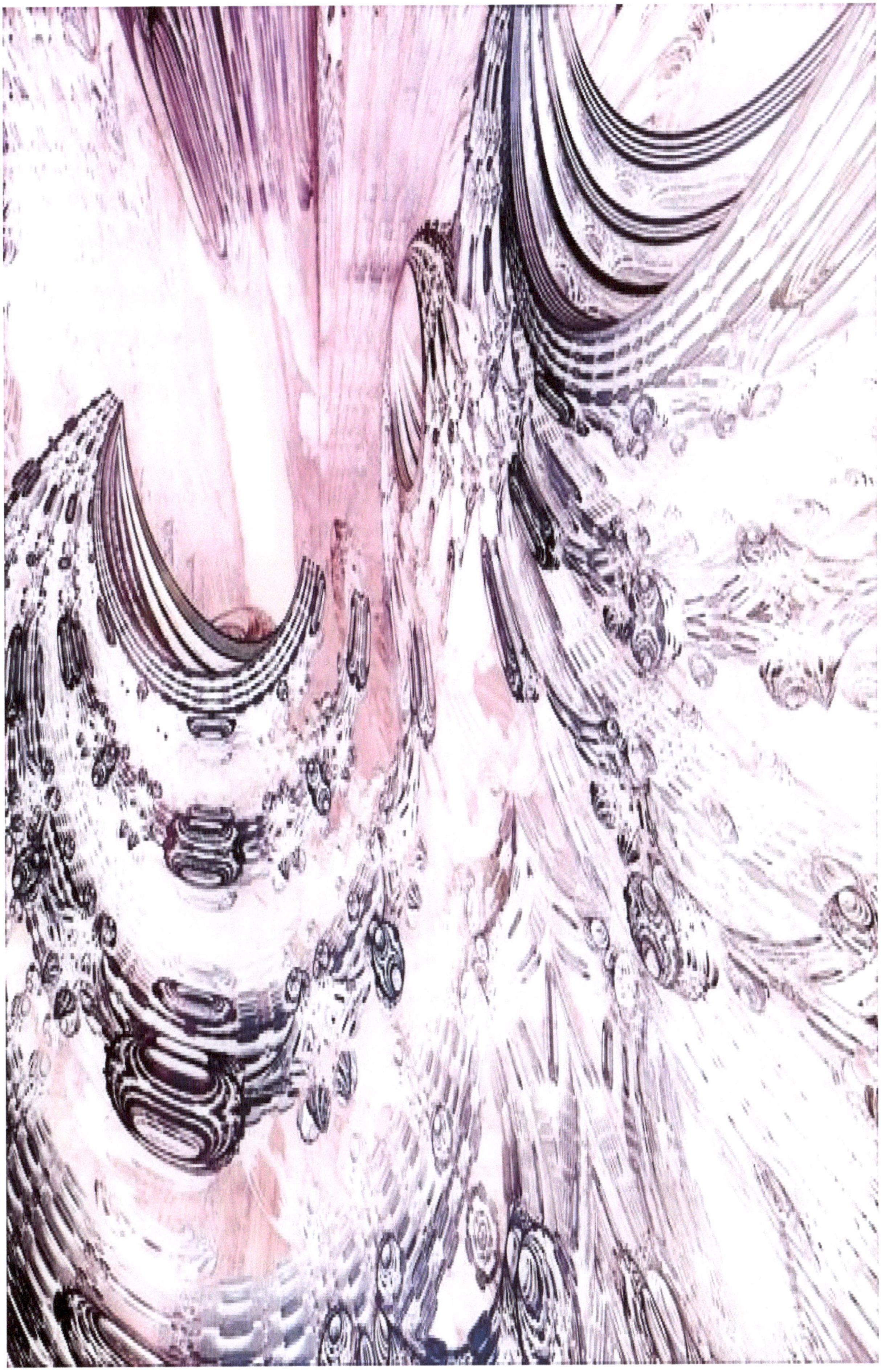

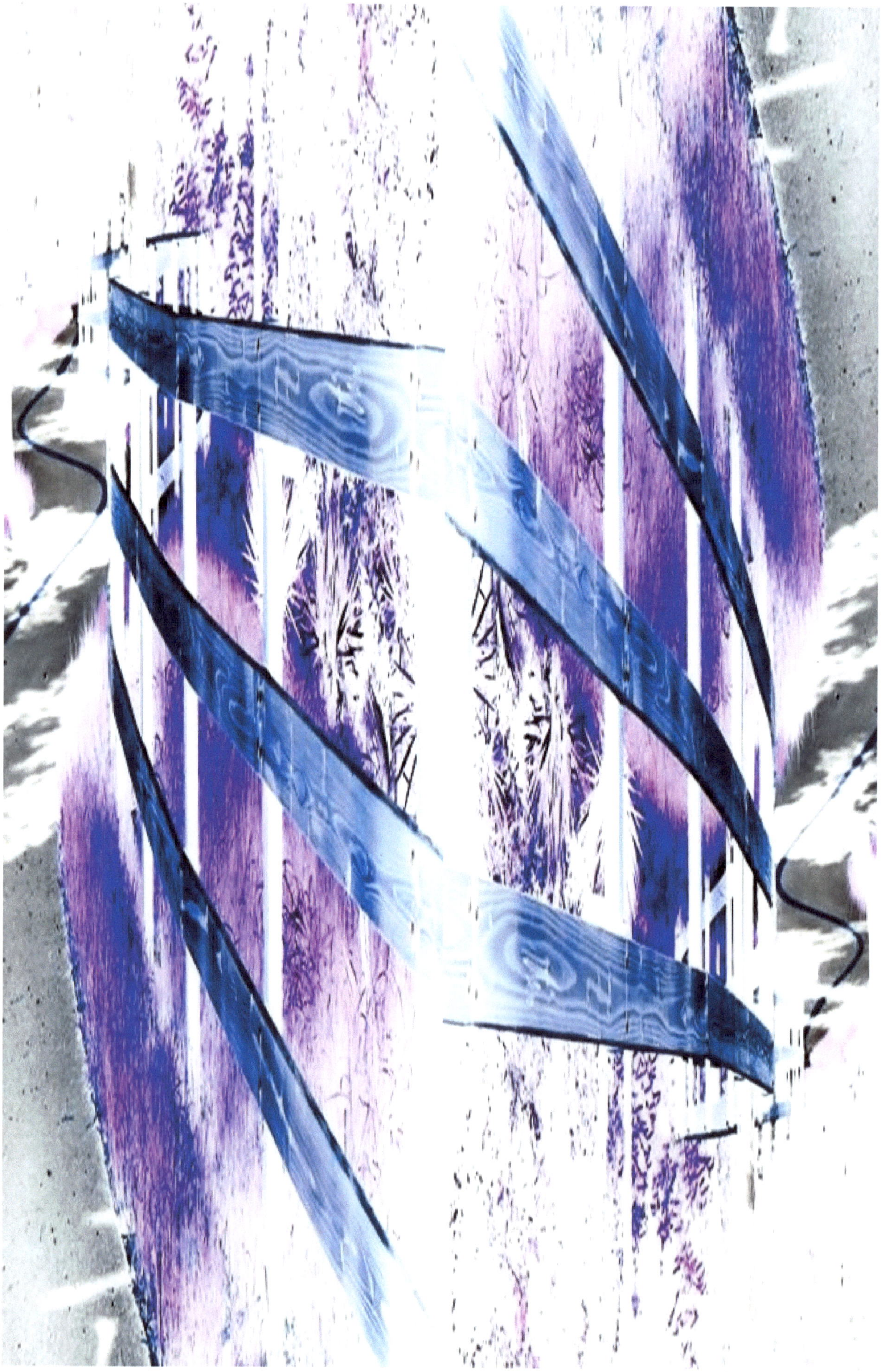

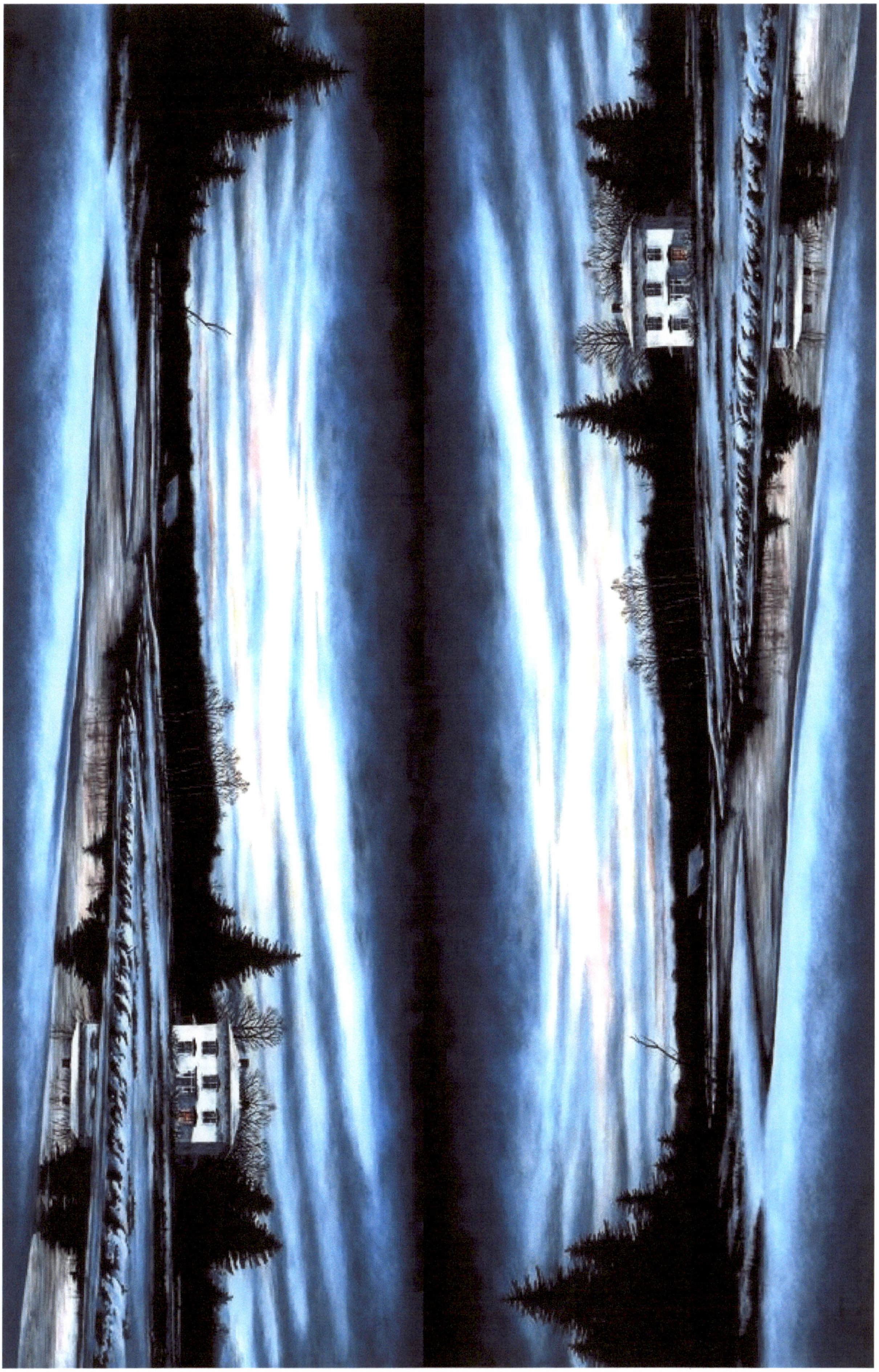

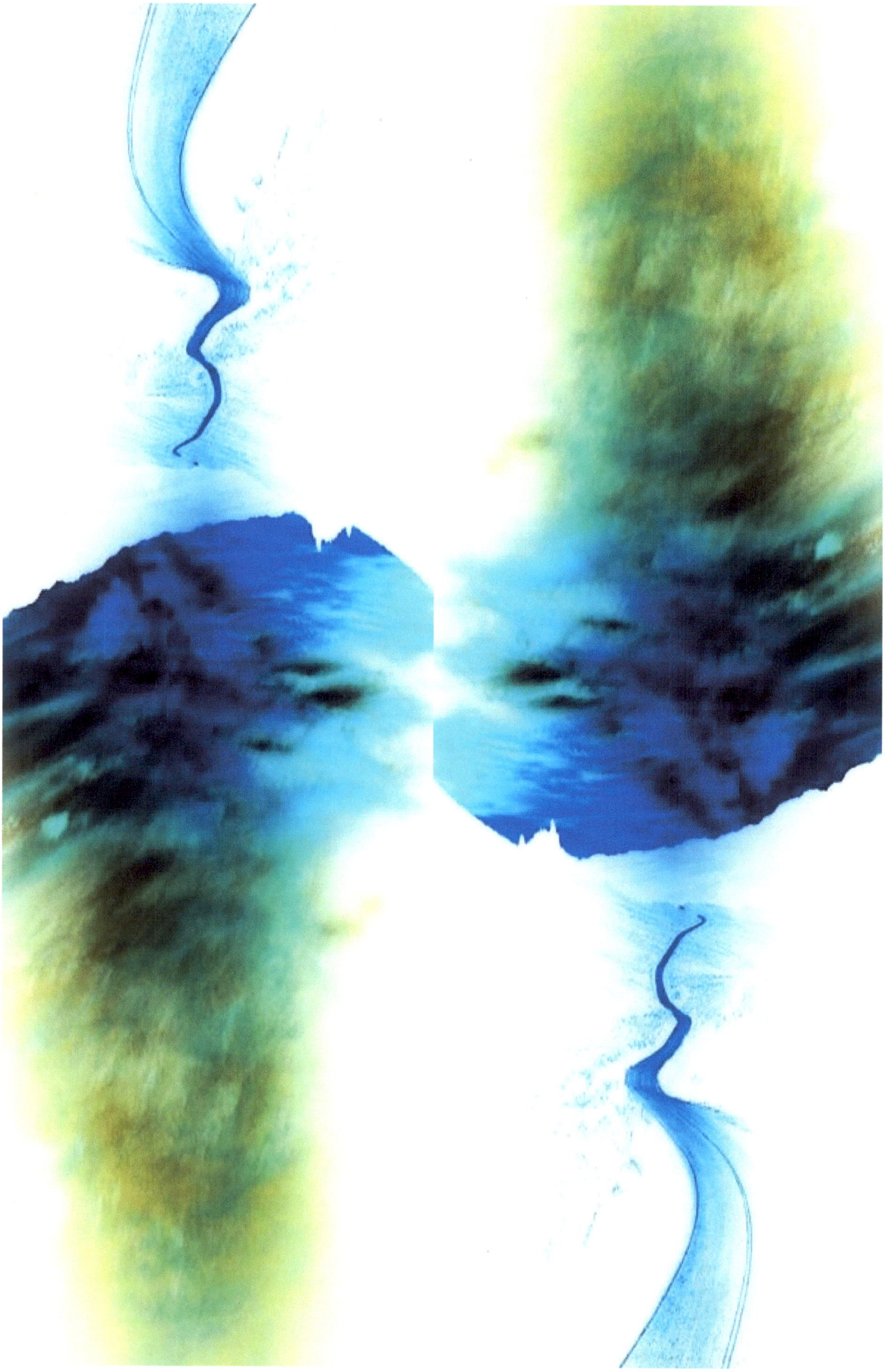

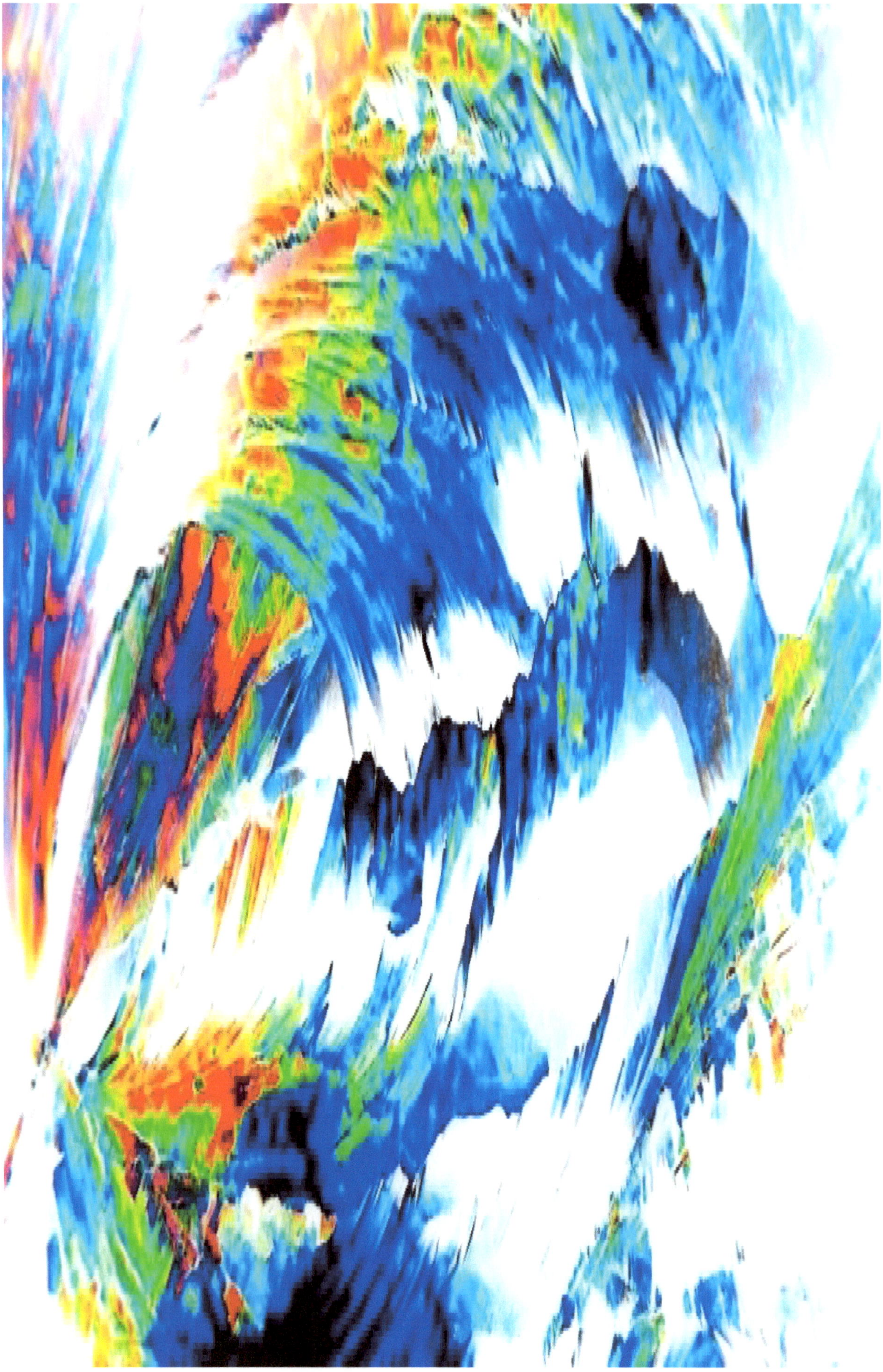

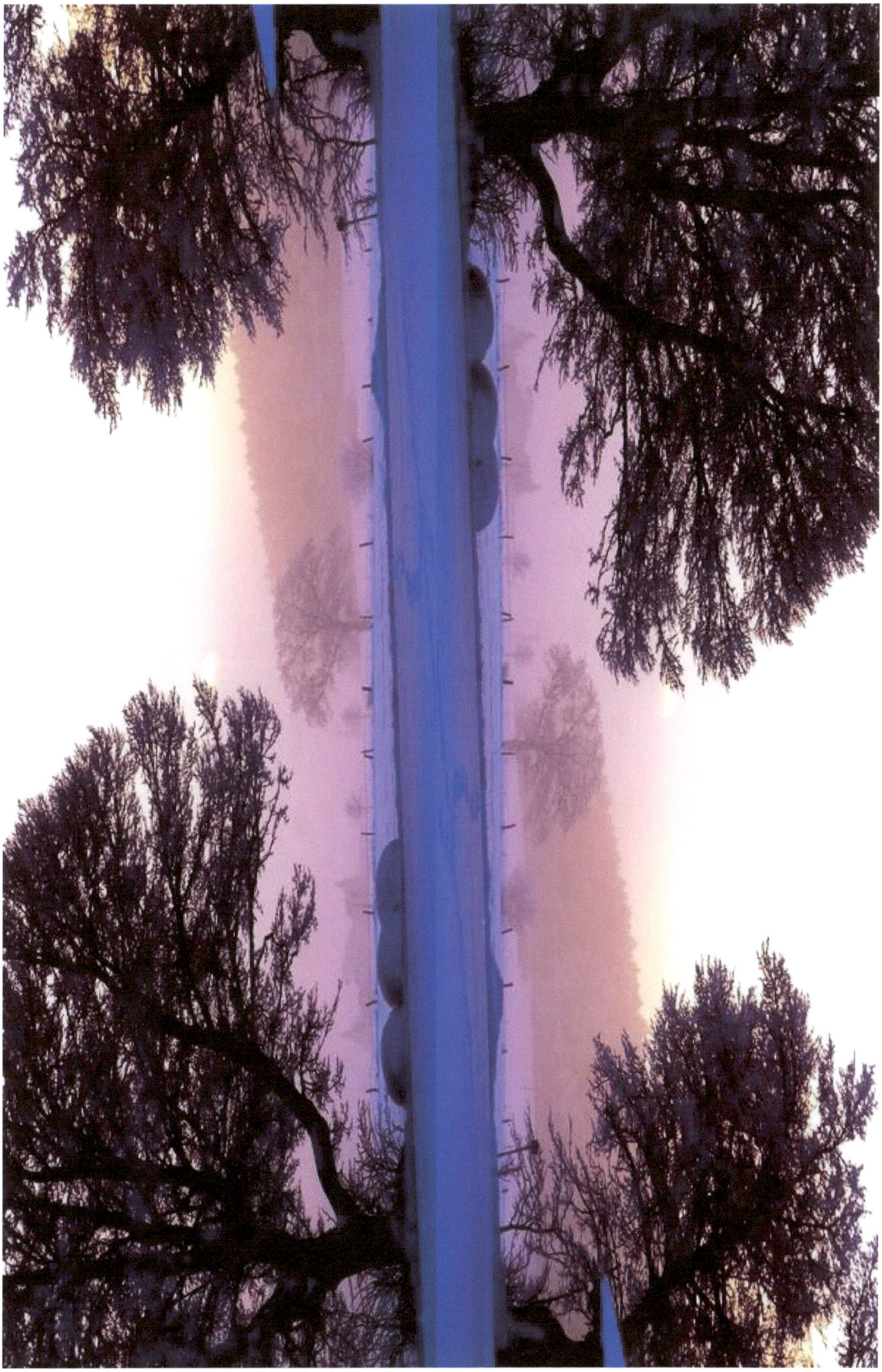

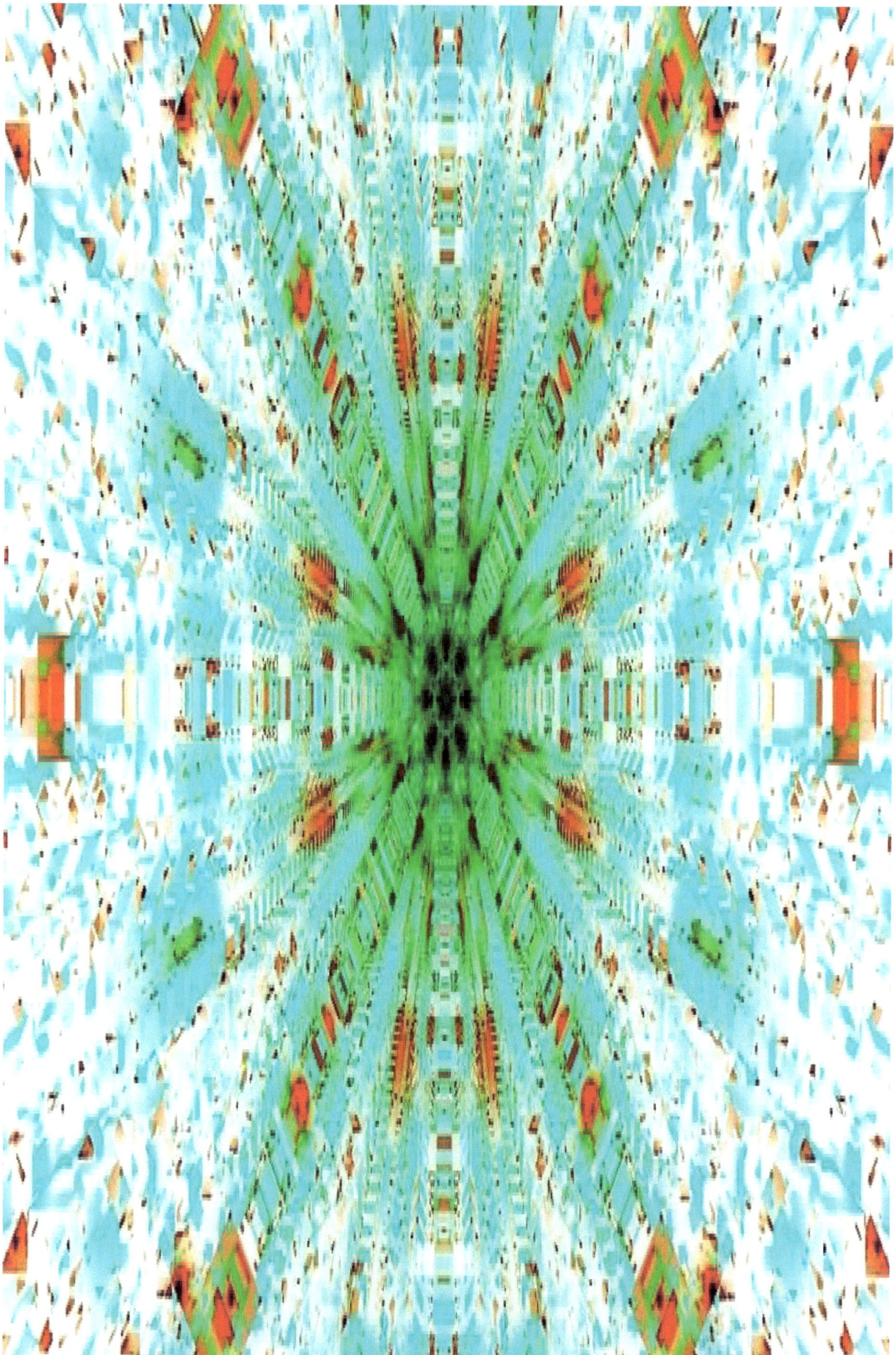

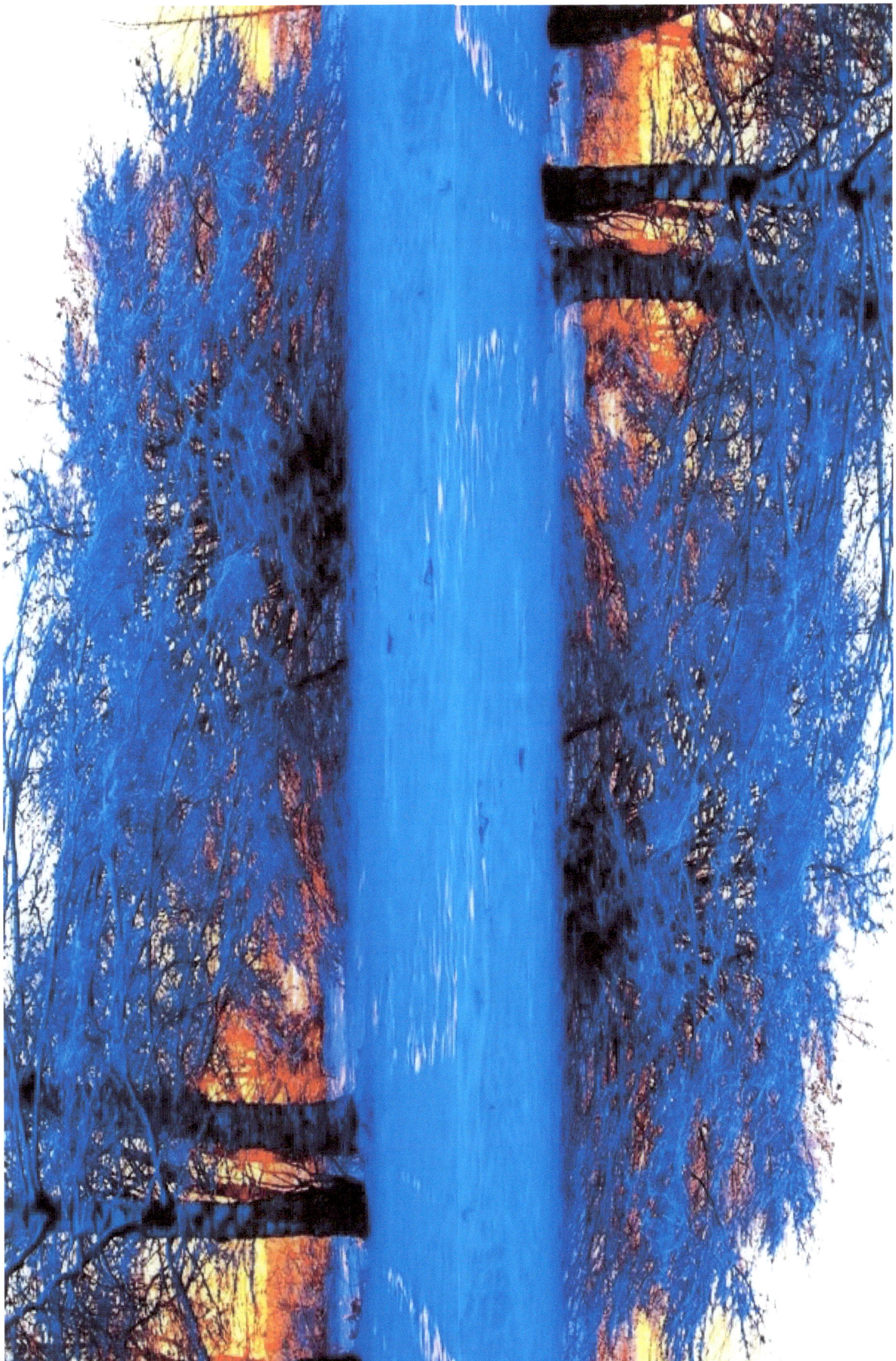

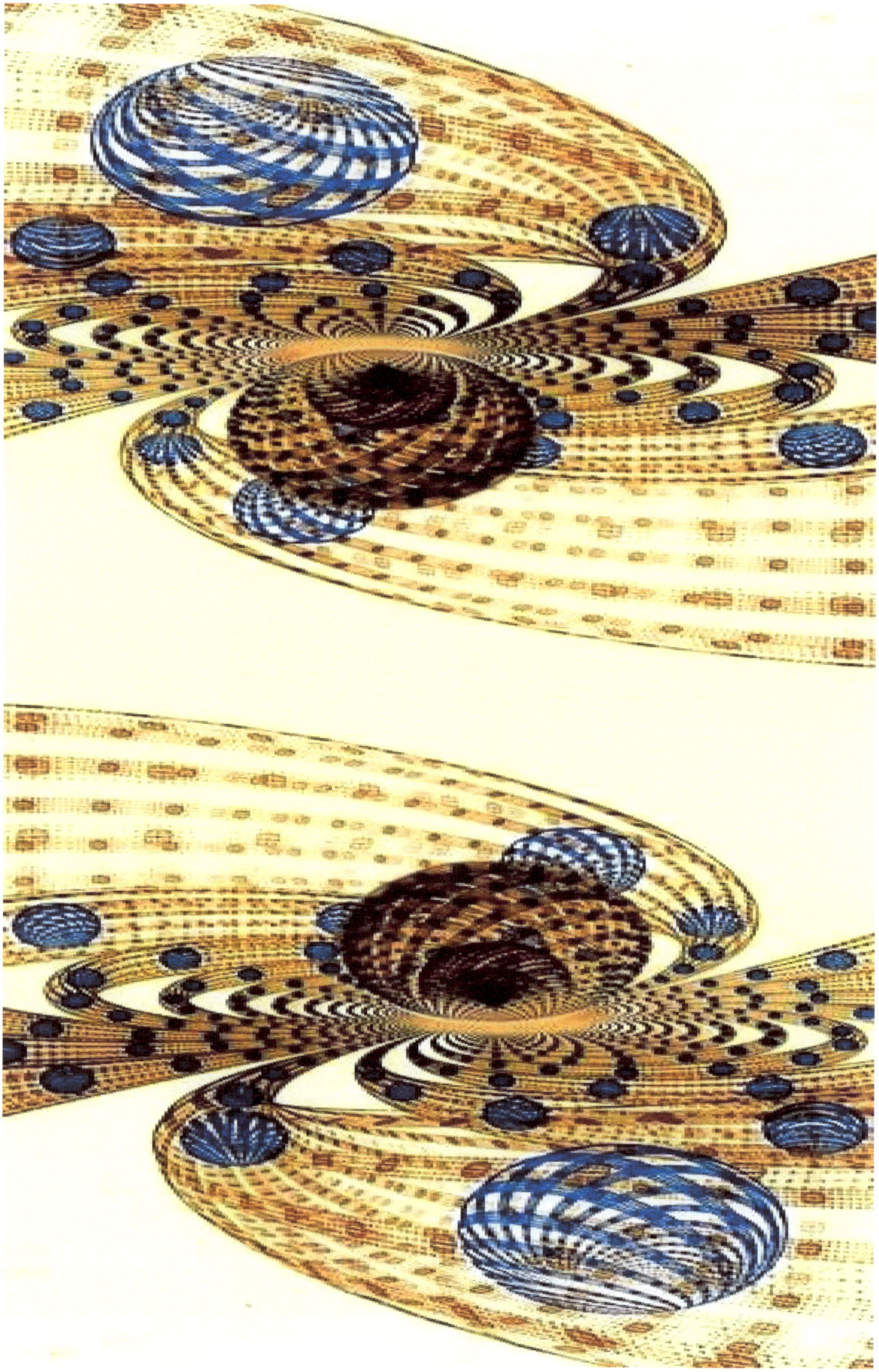

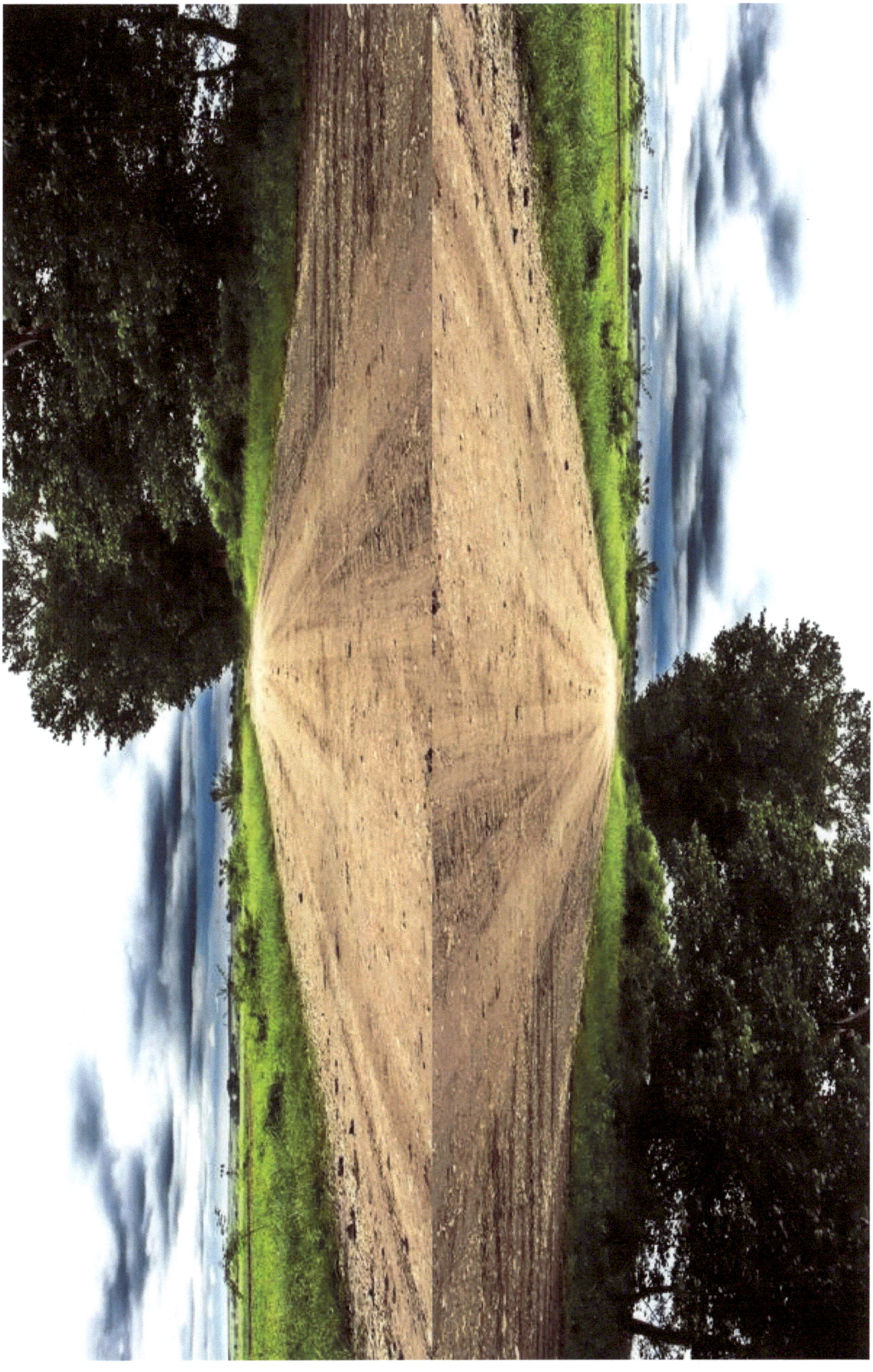

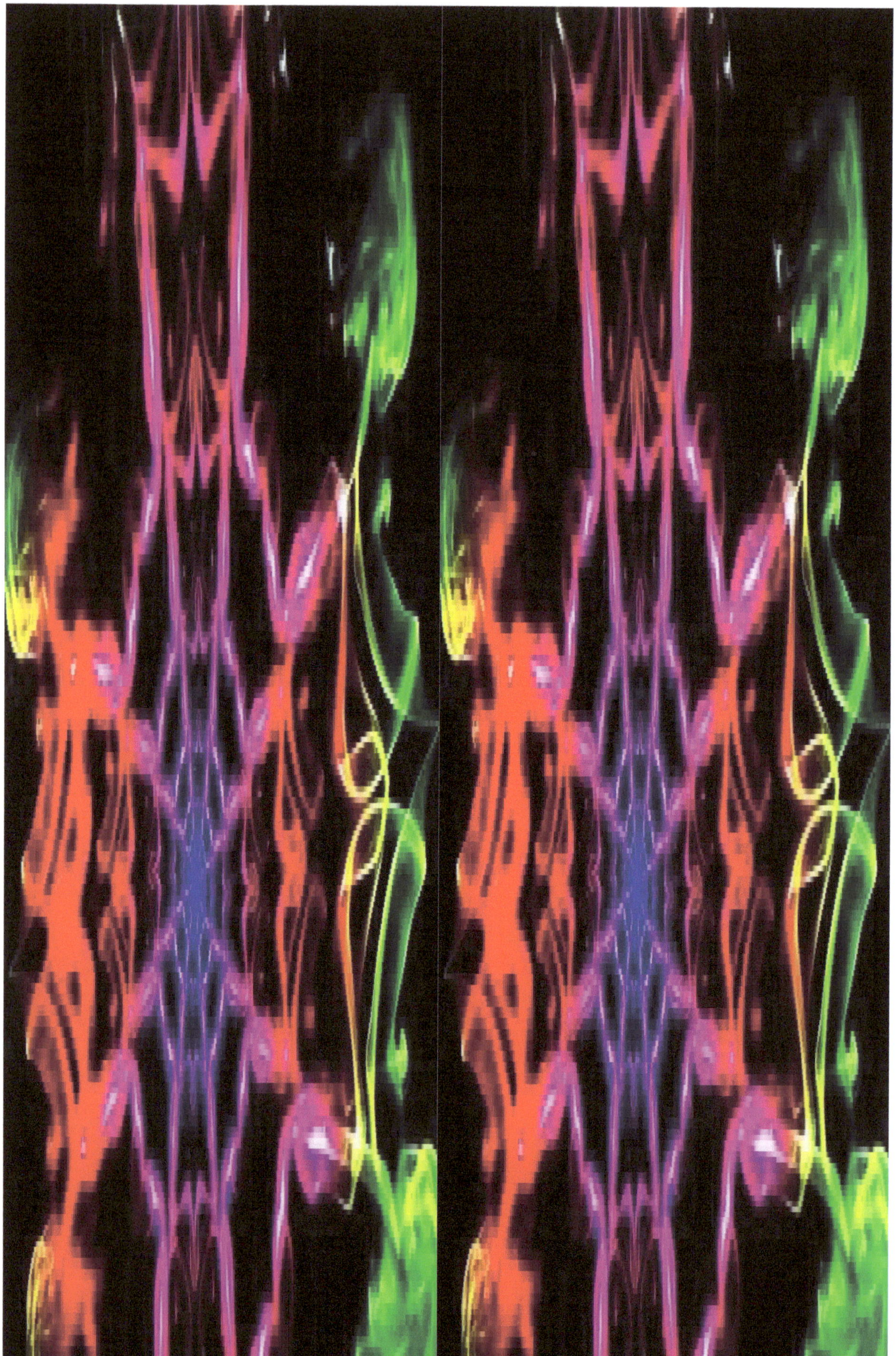

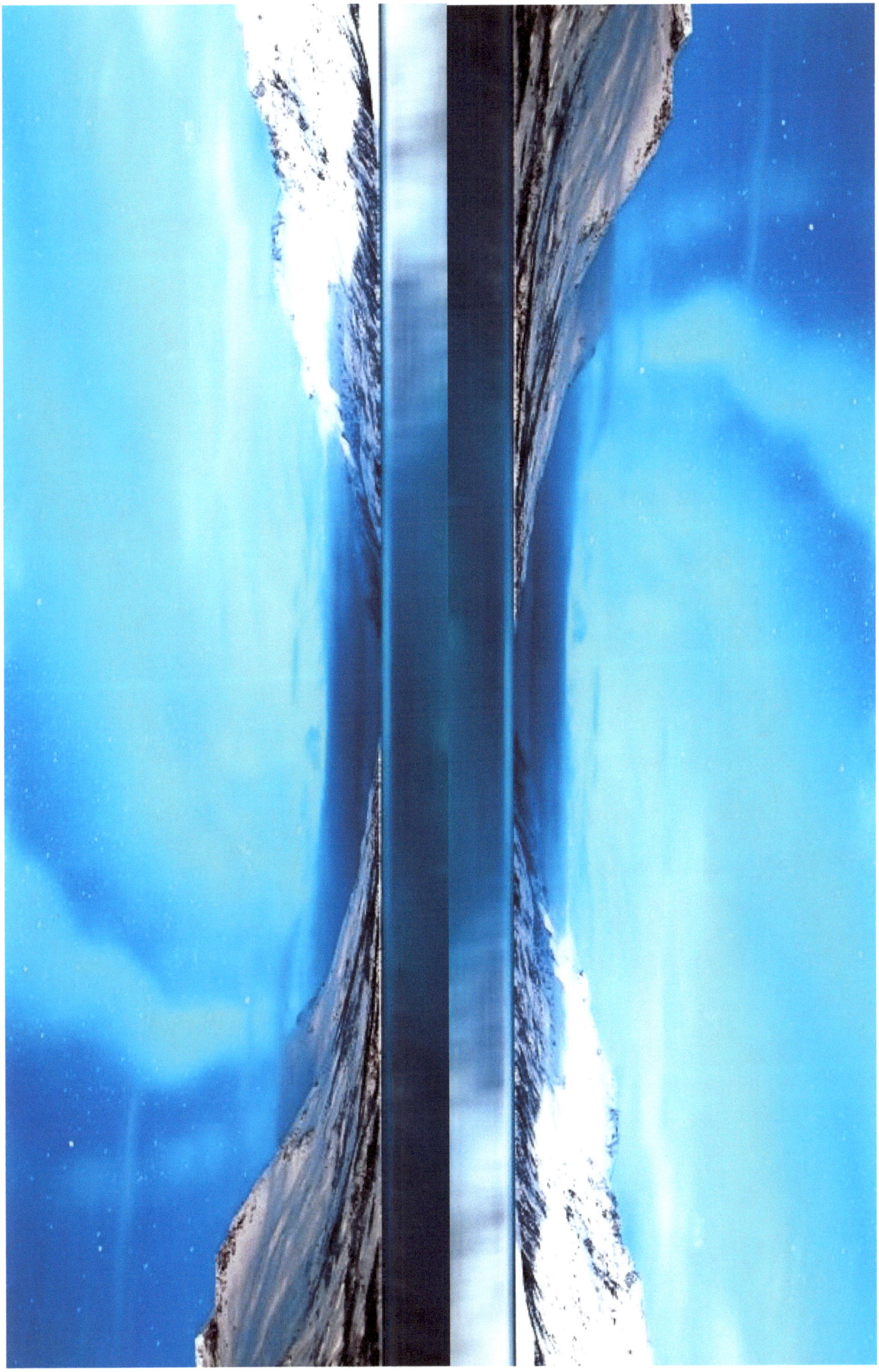

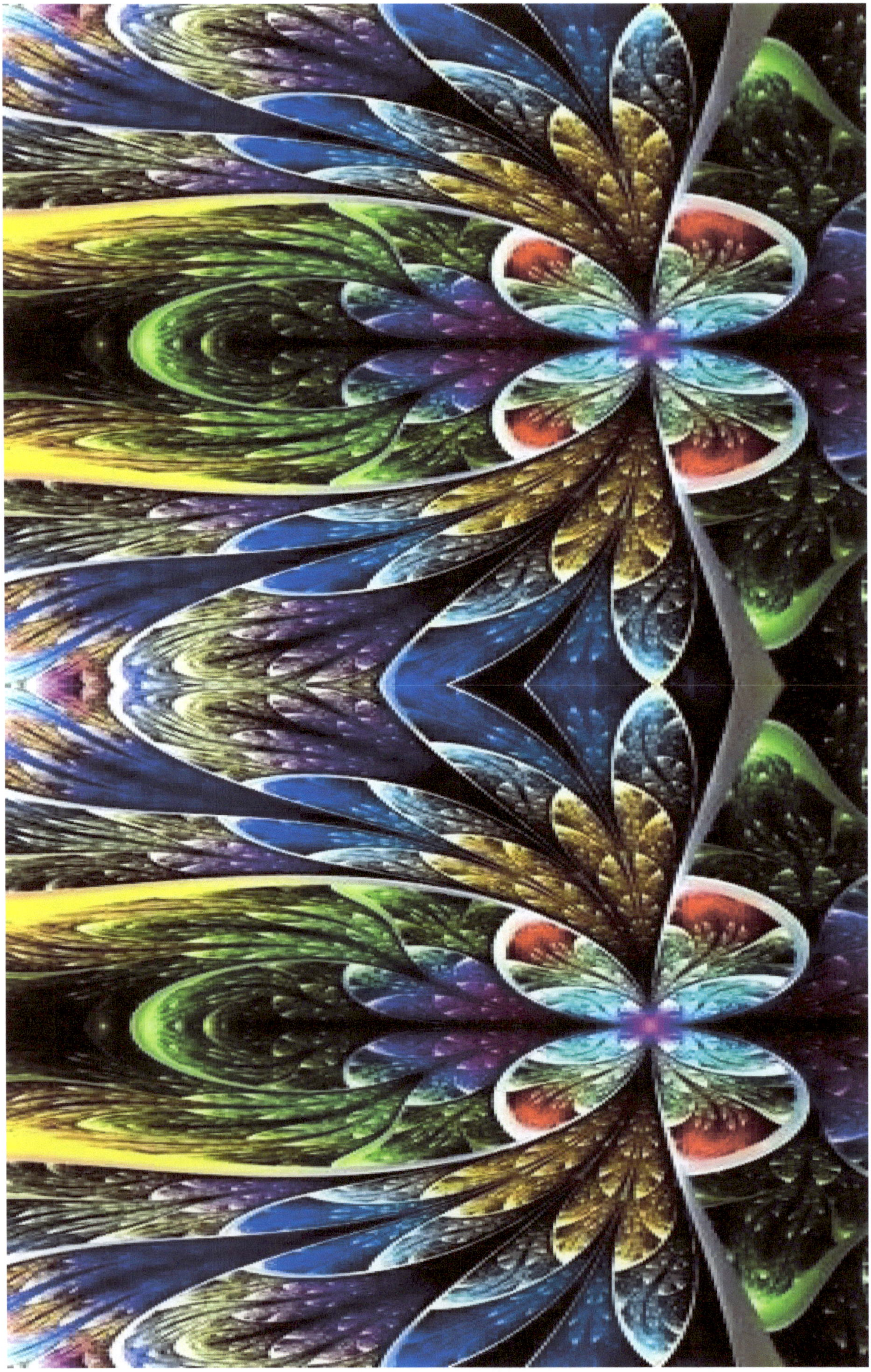

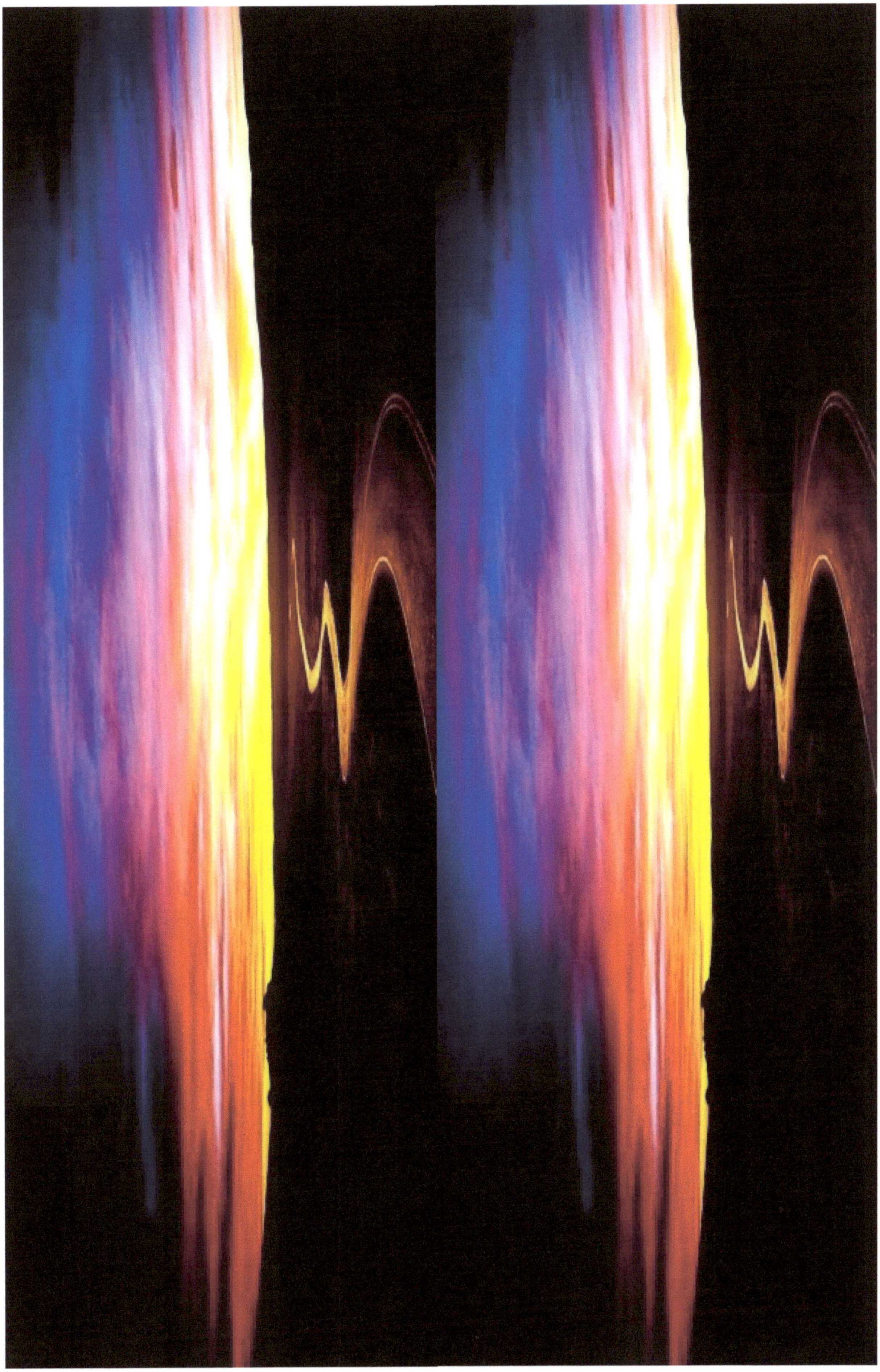

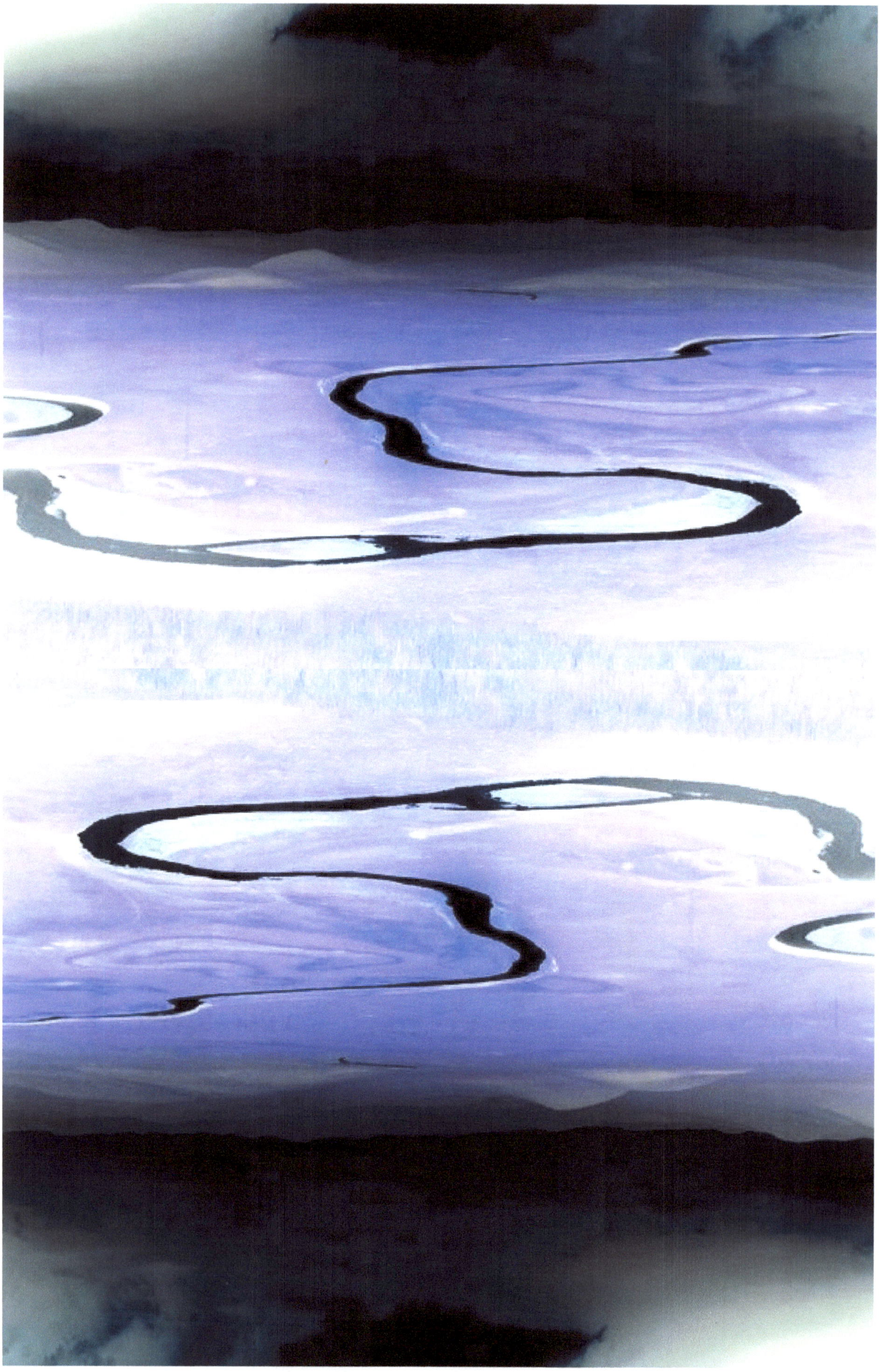

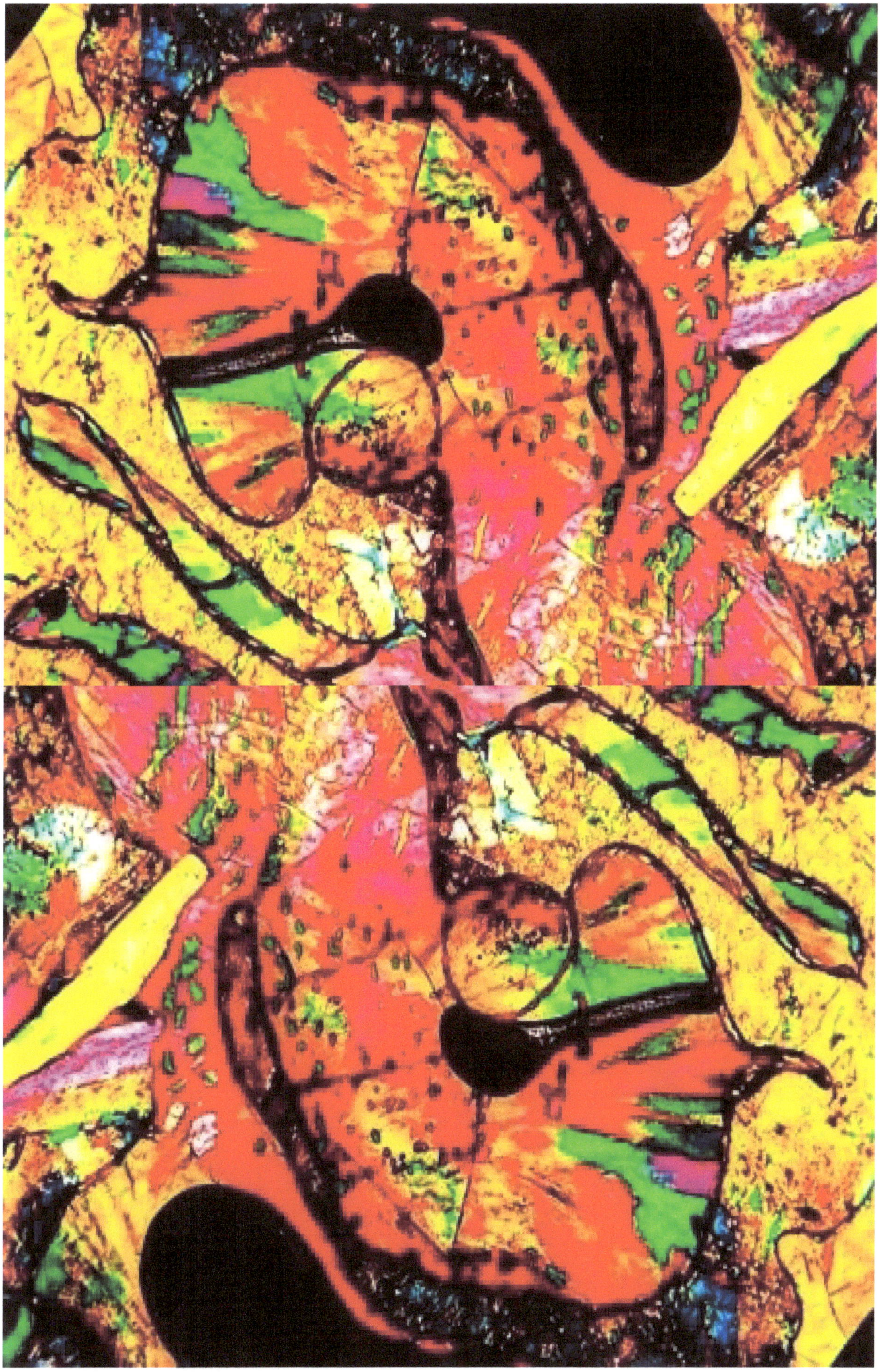

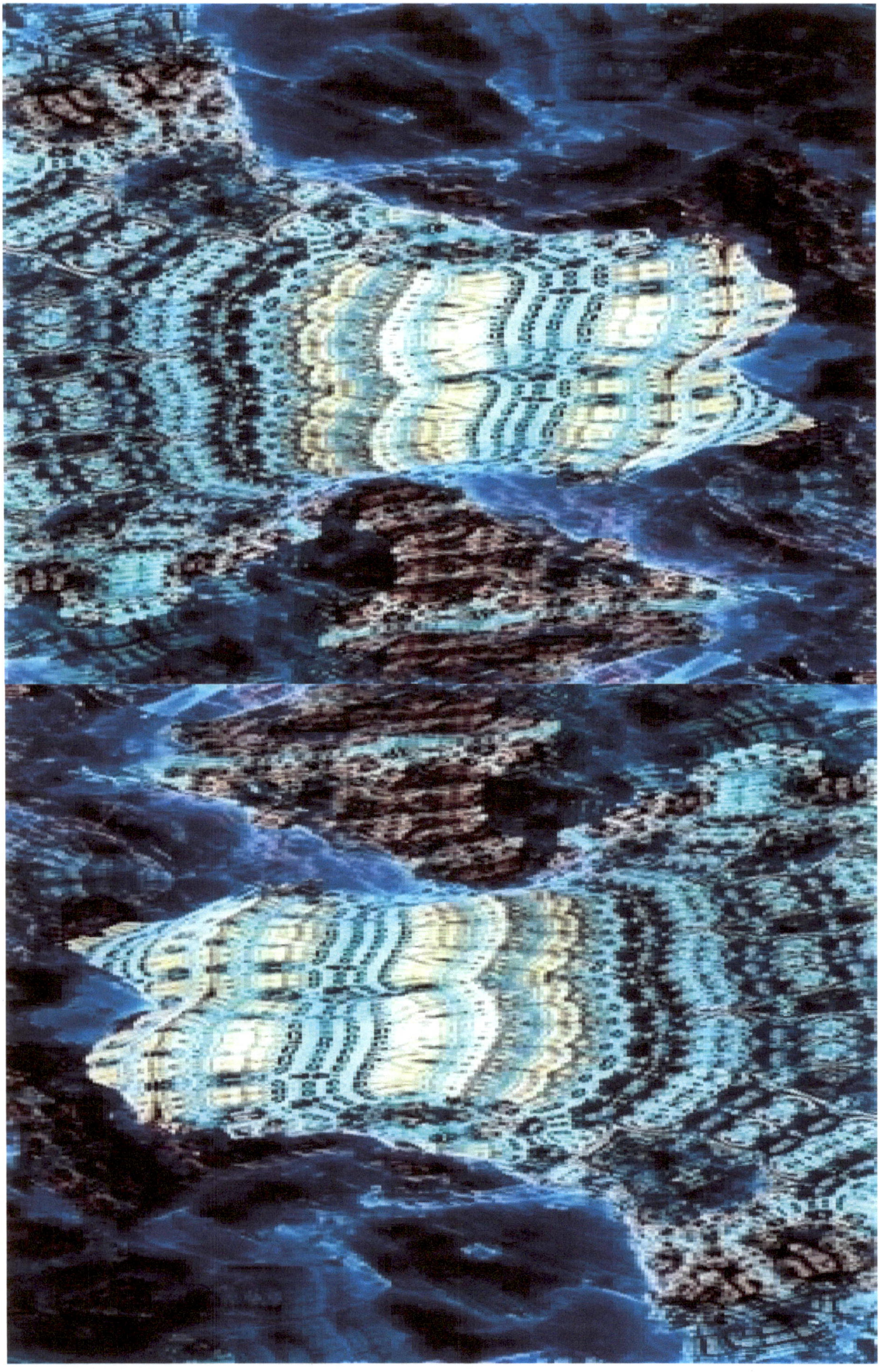

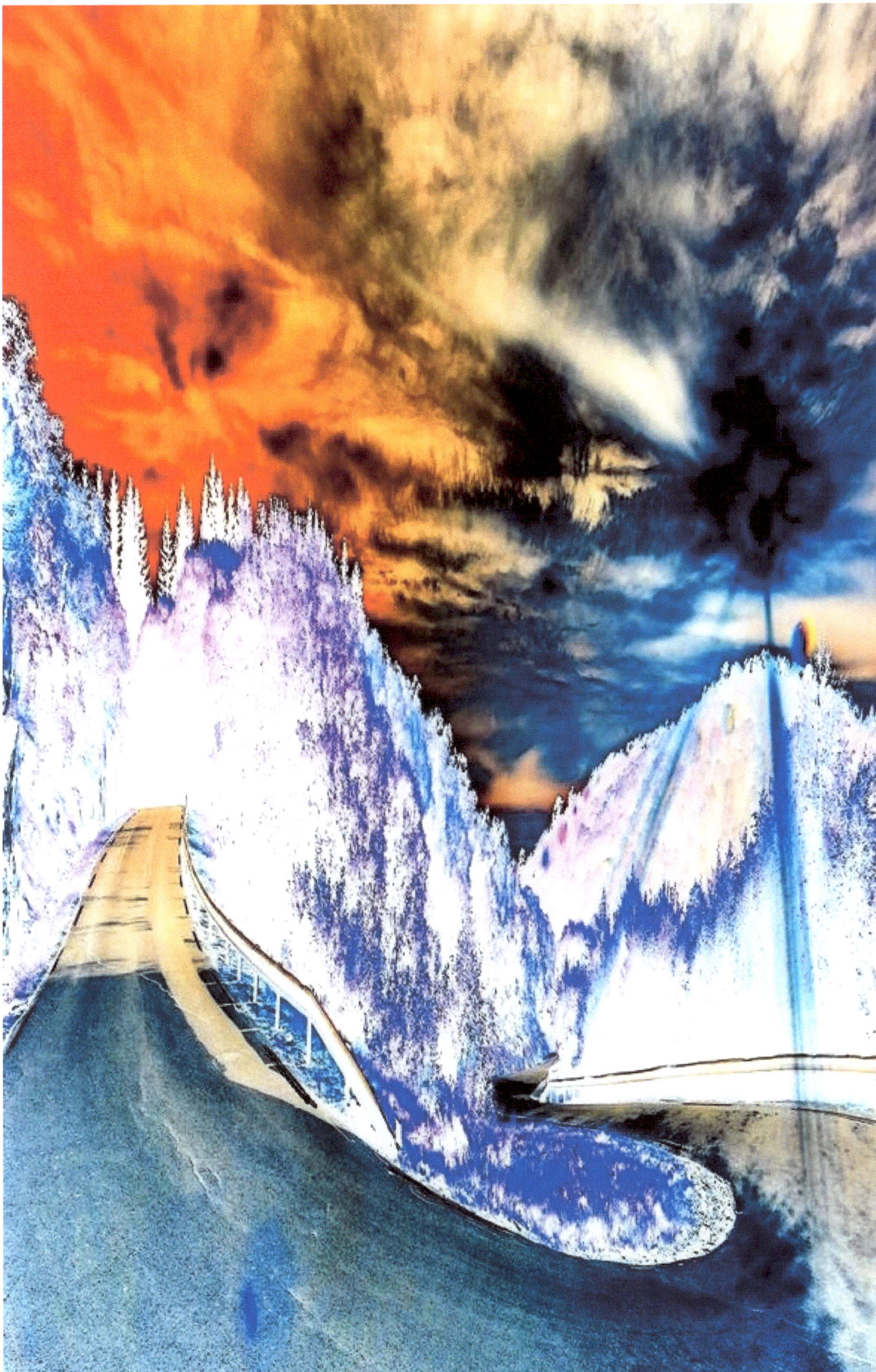

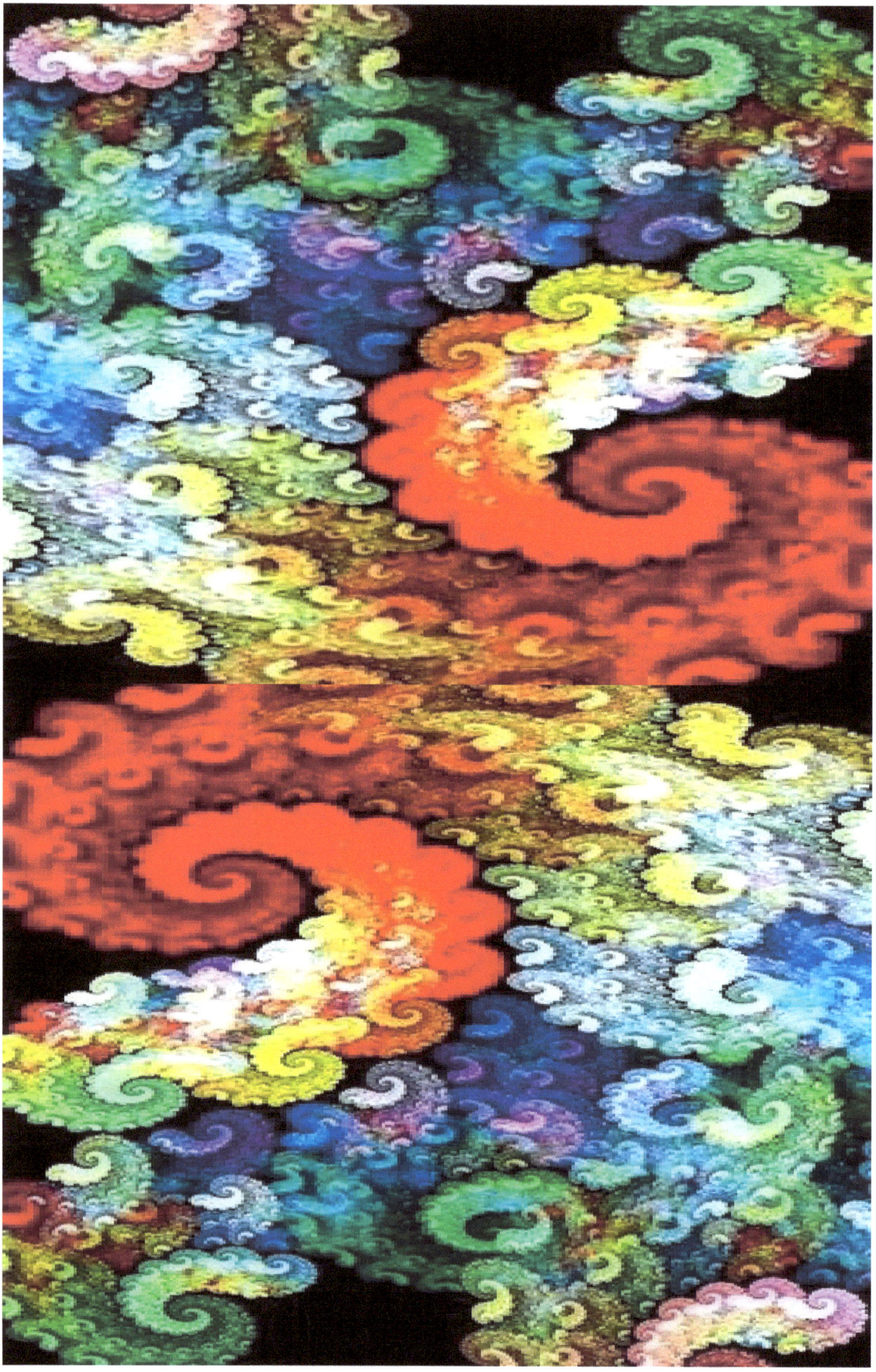

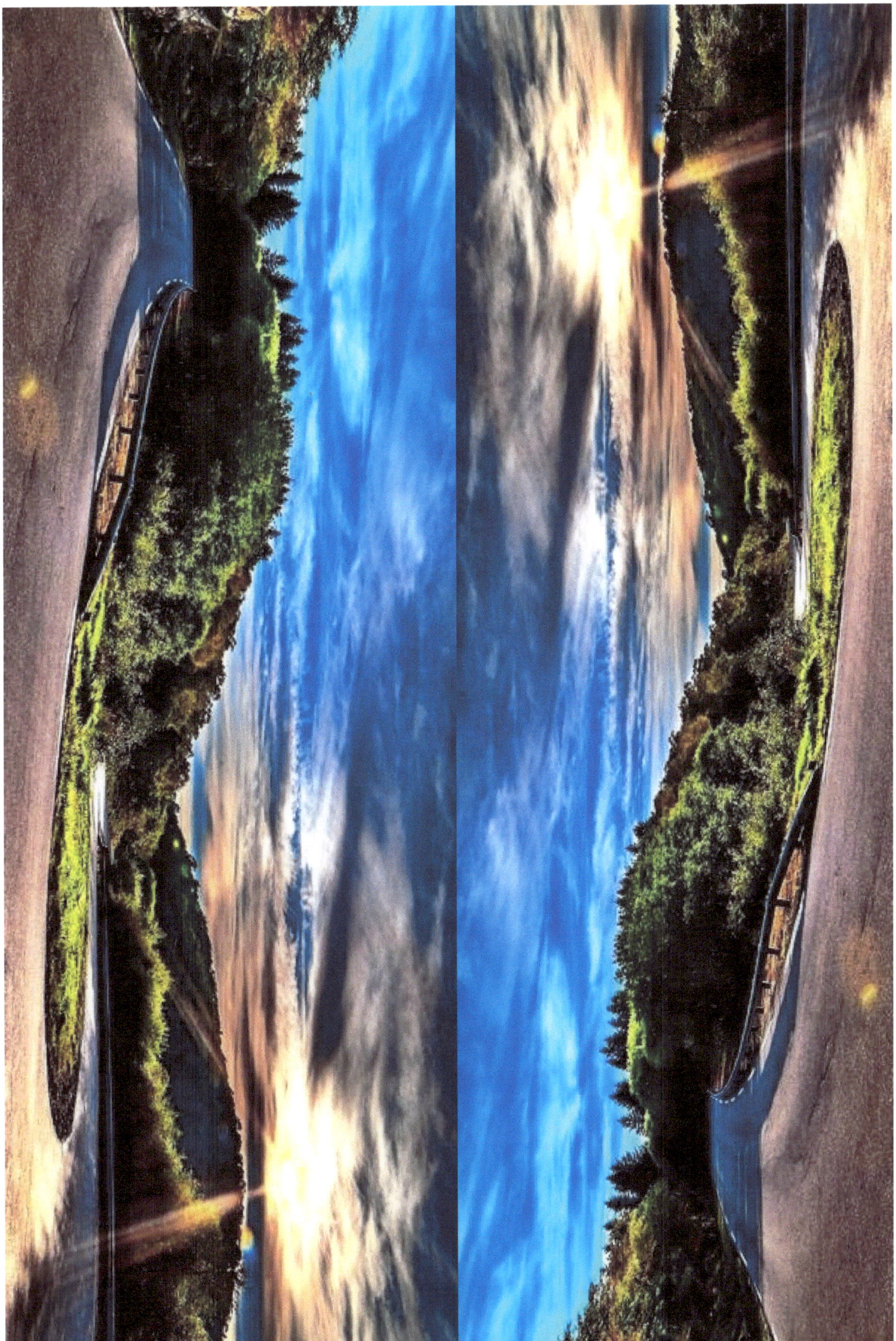

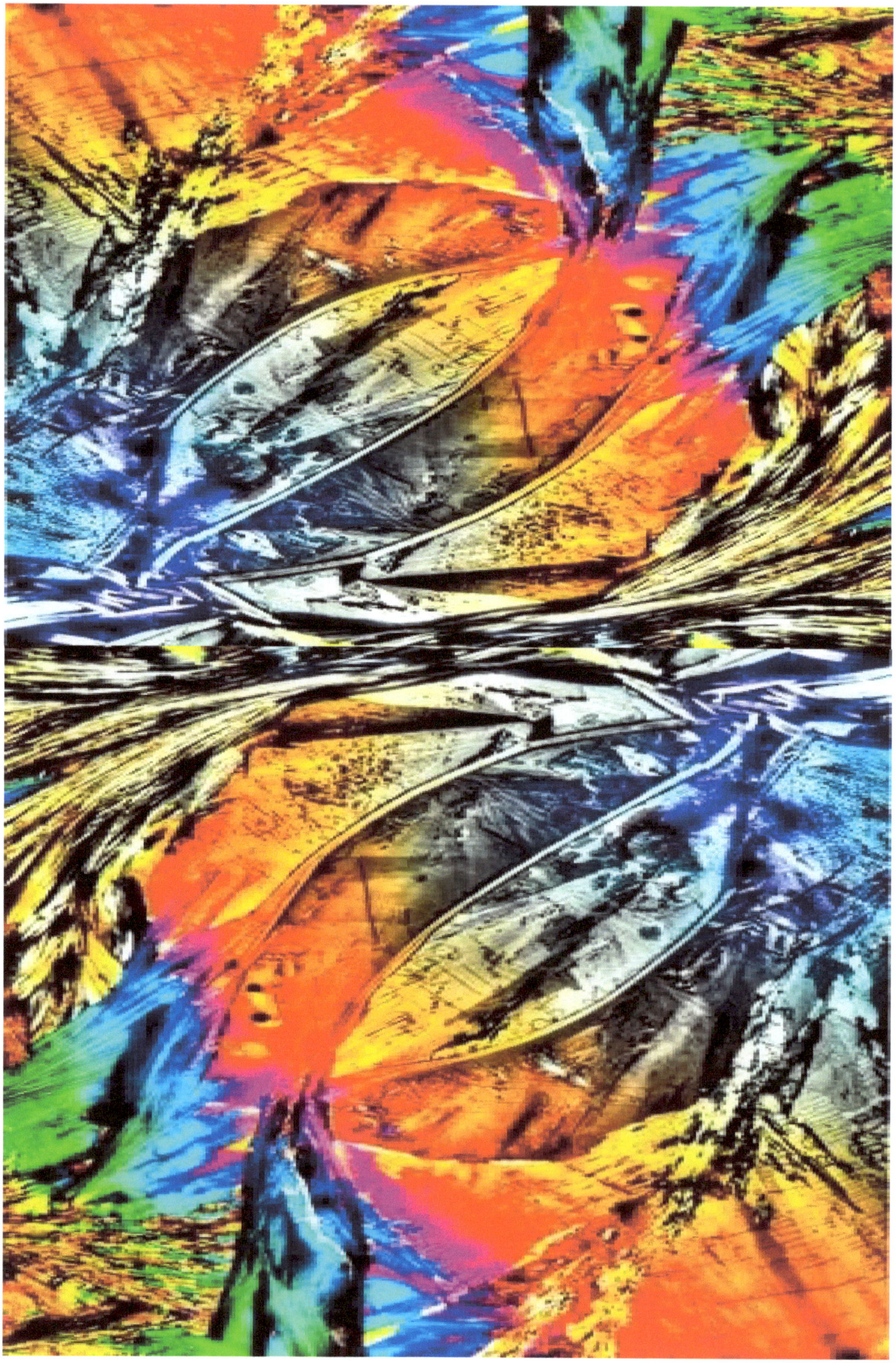

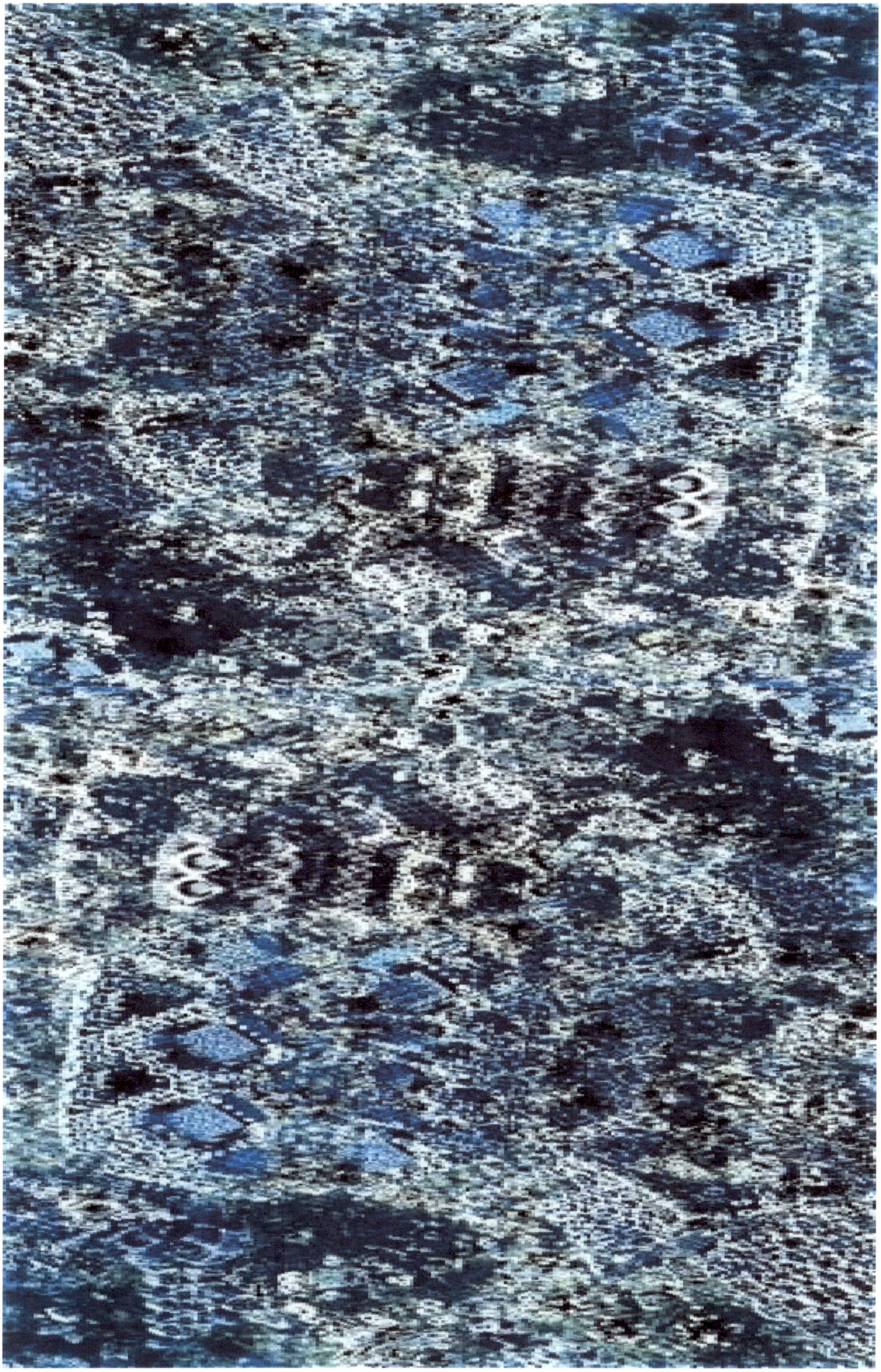

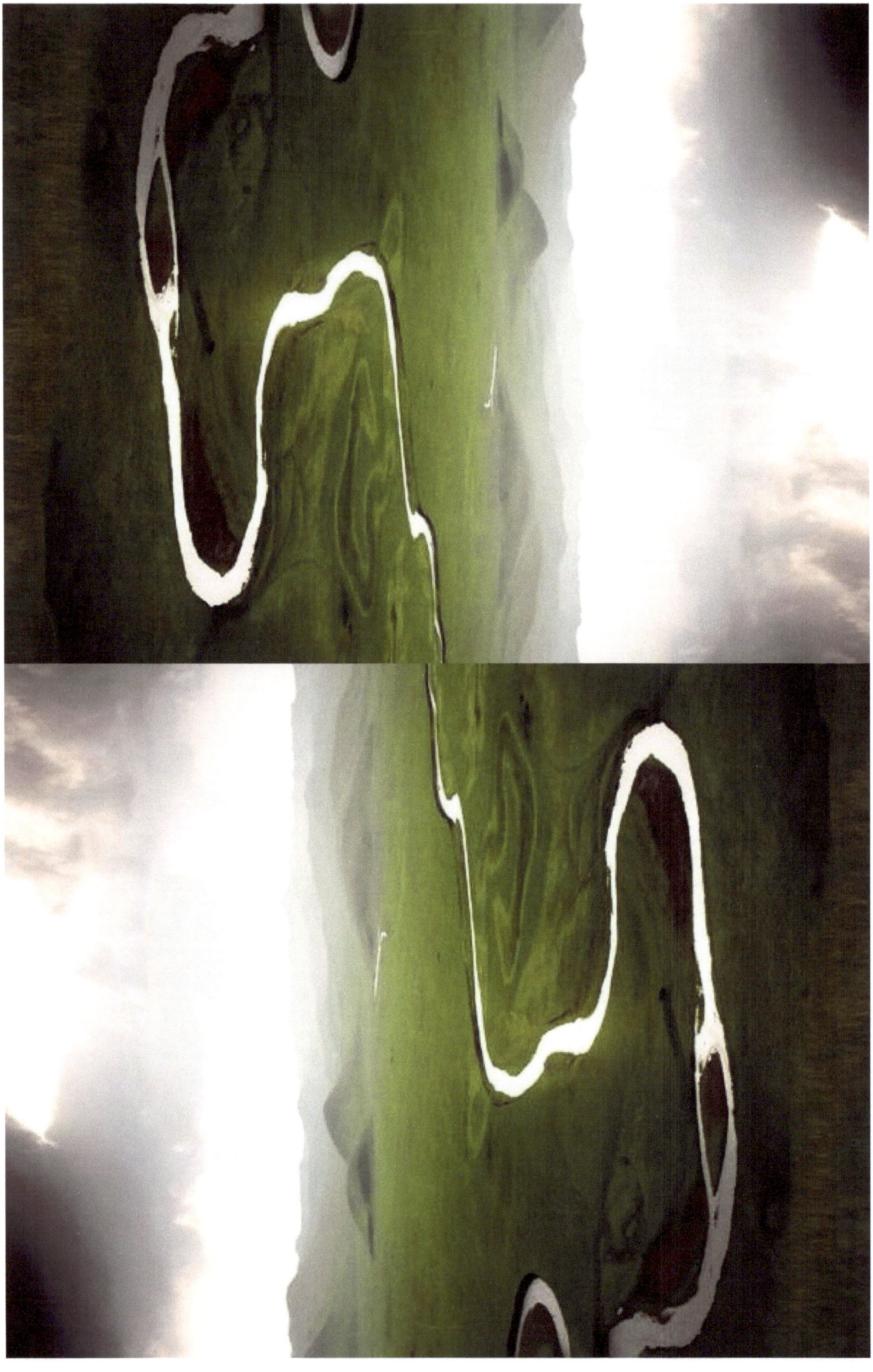

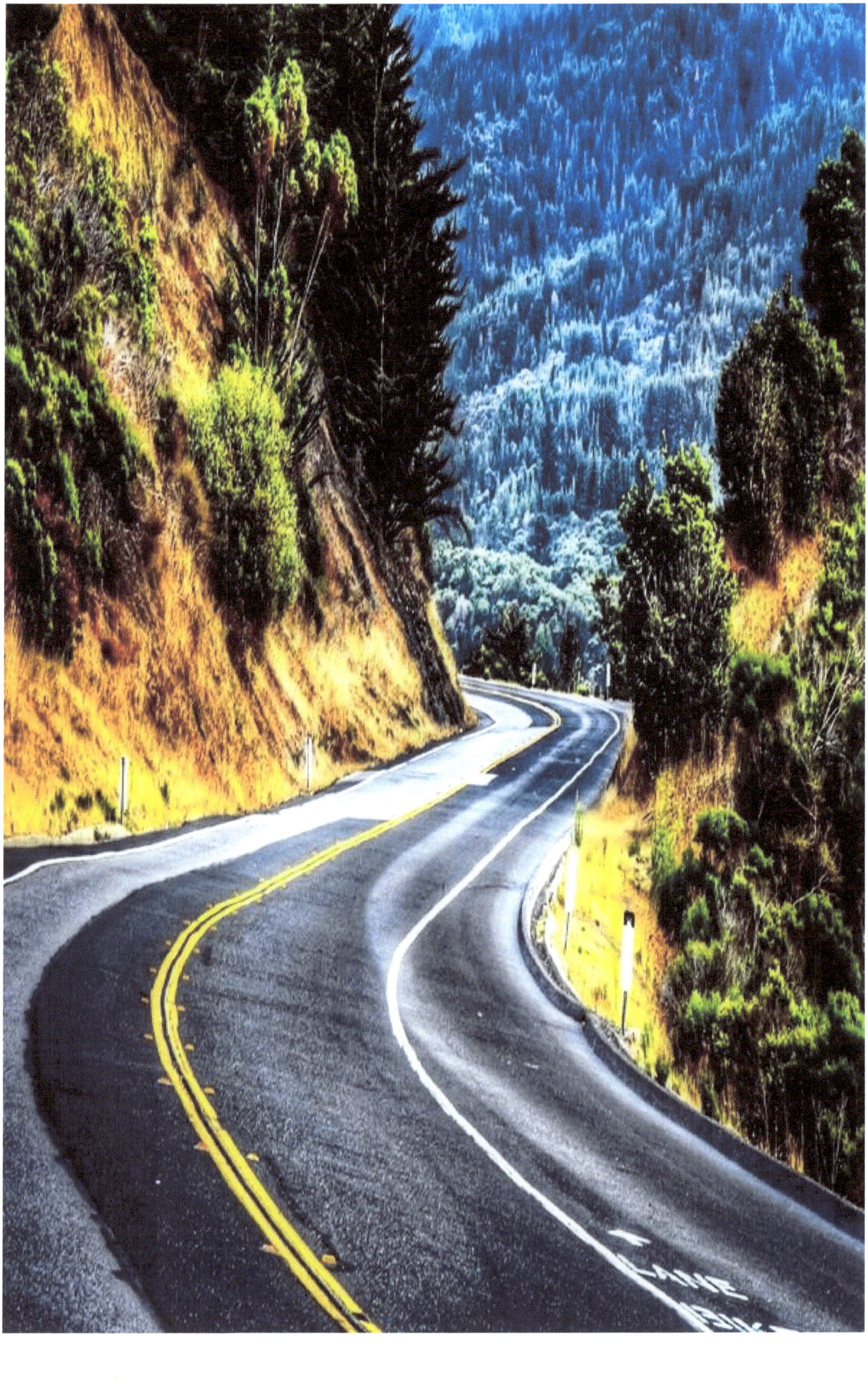
LANE

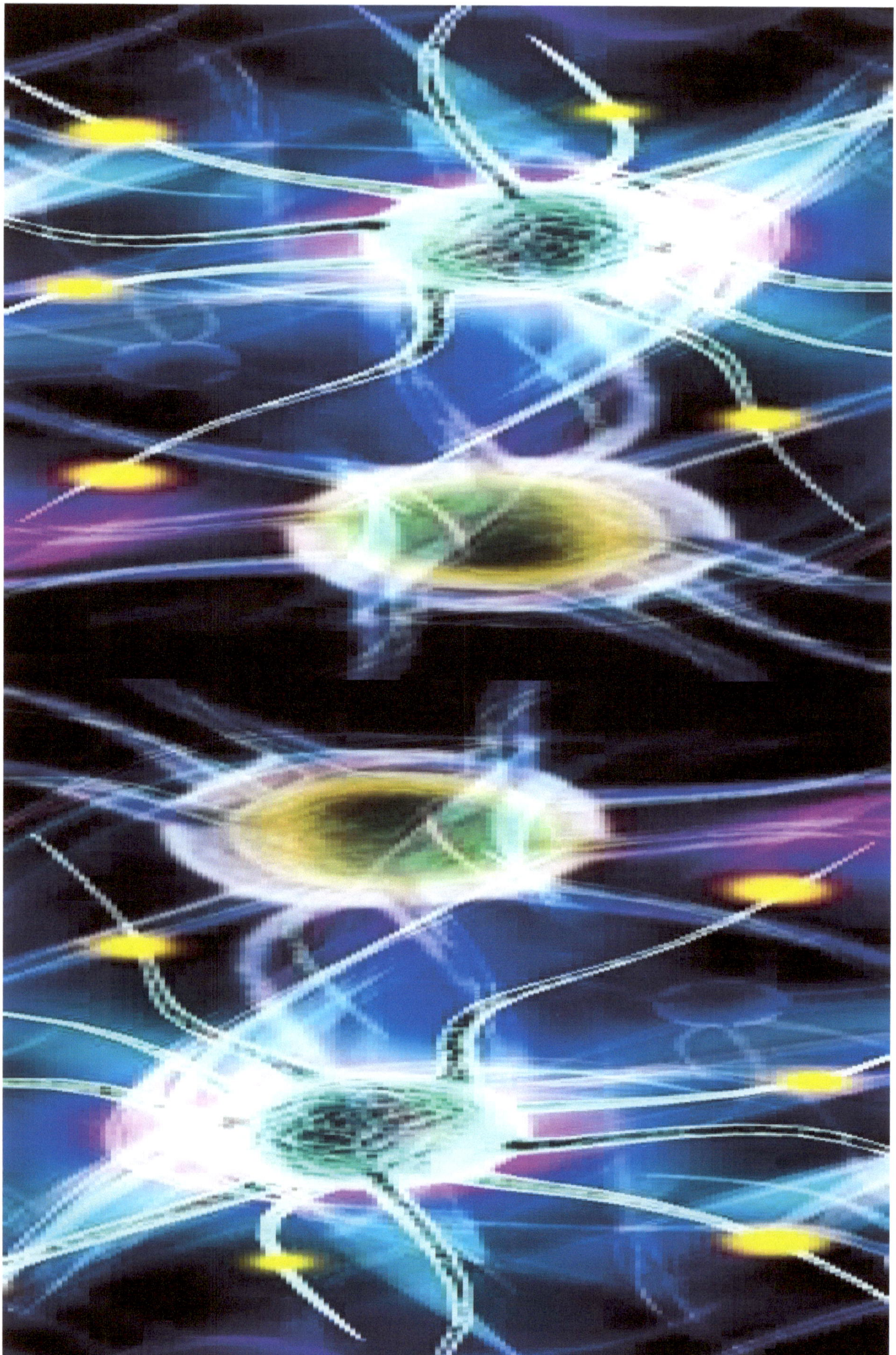

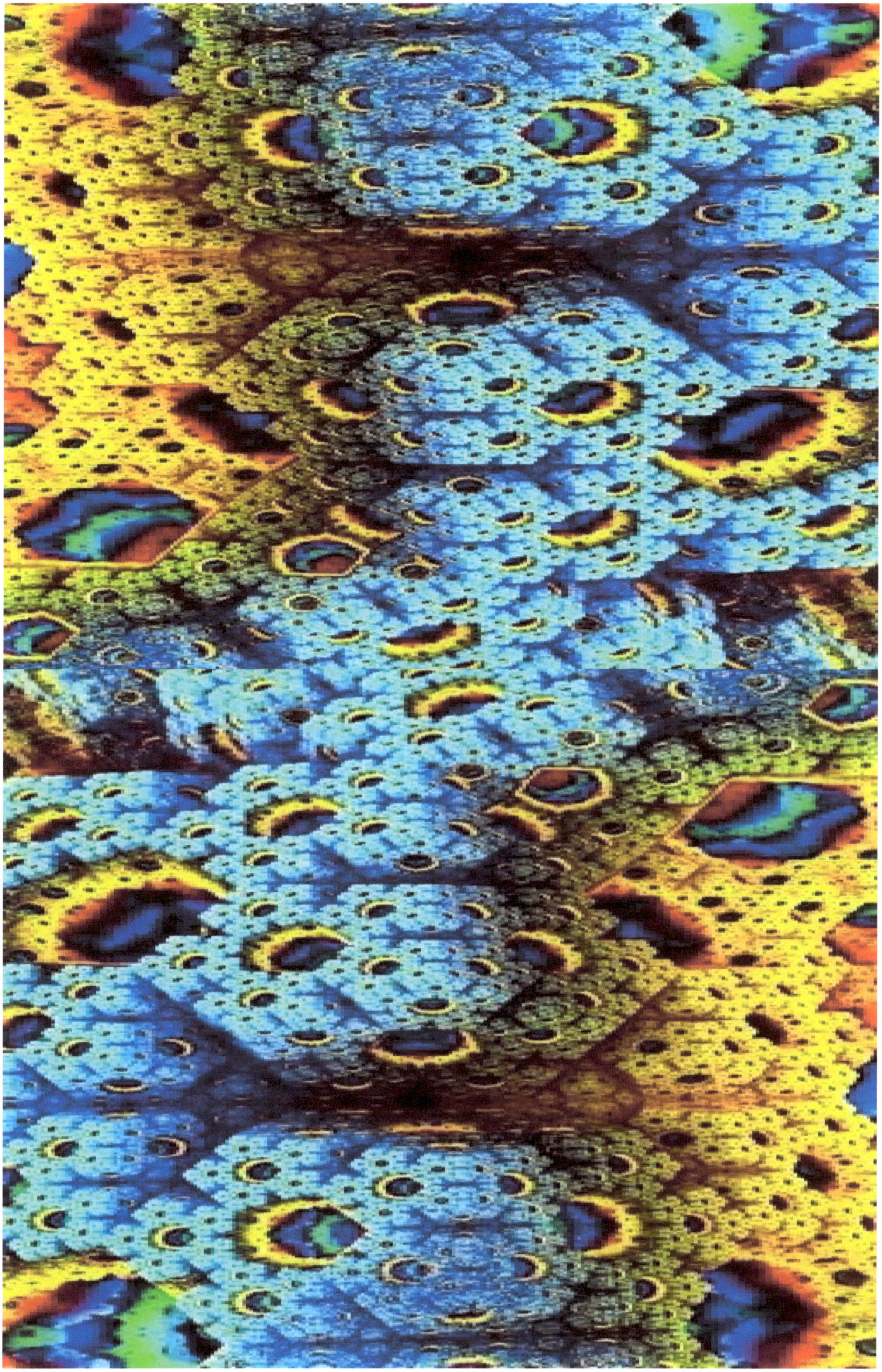

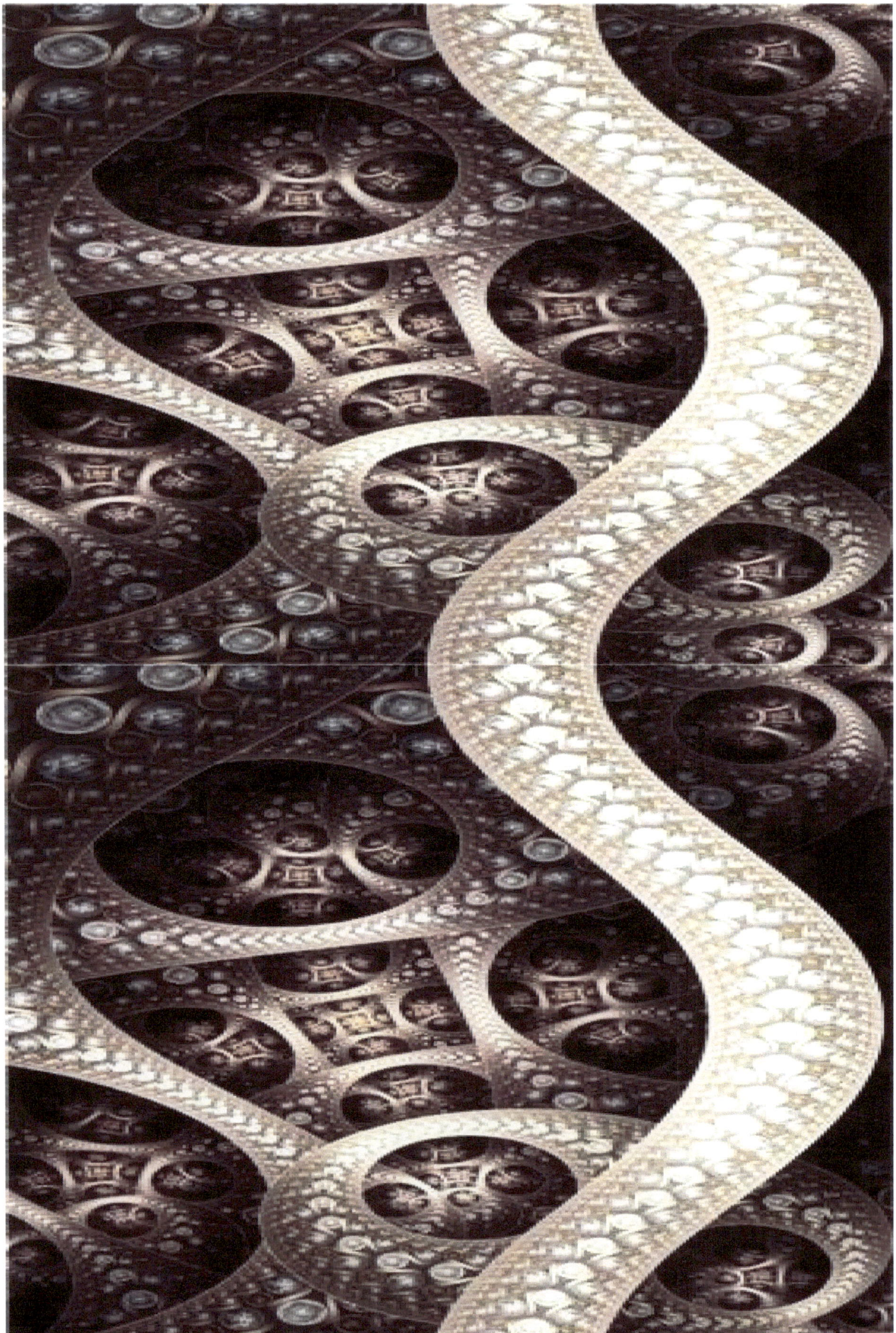

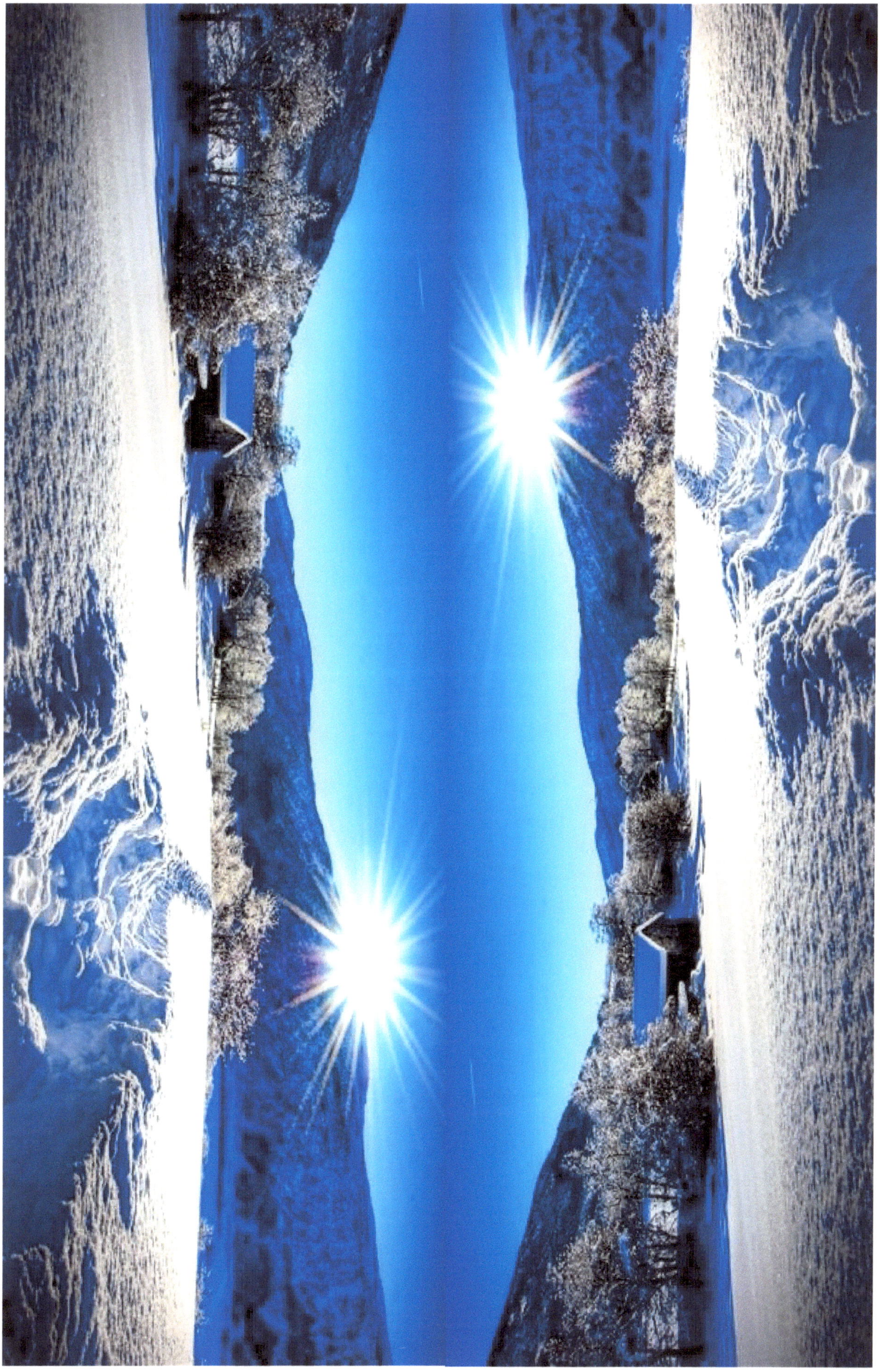

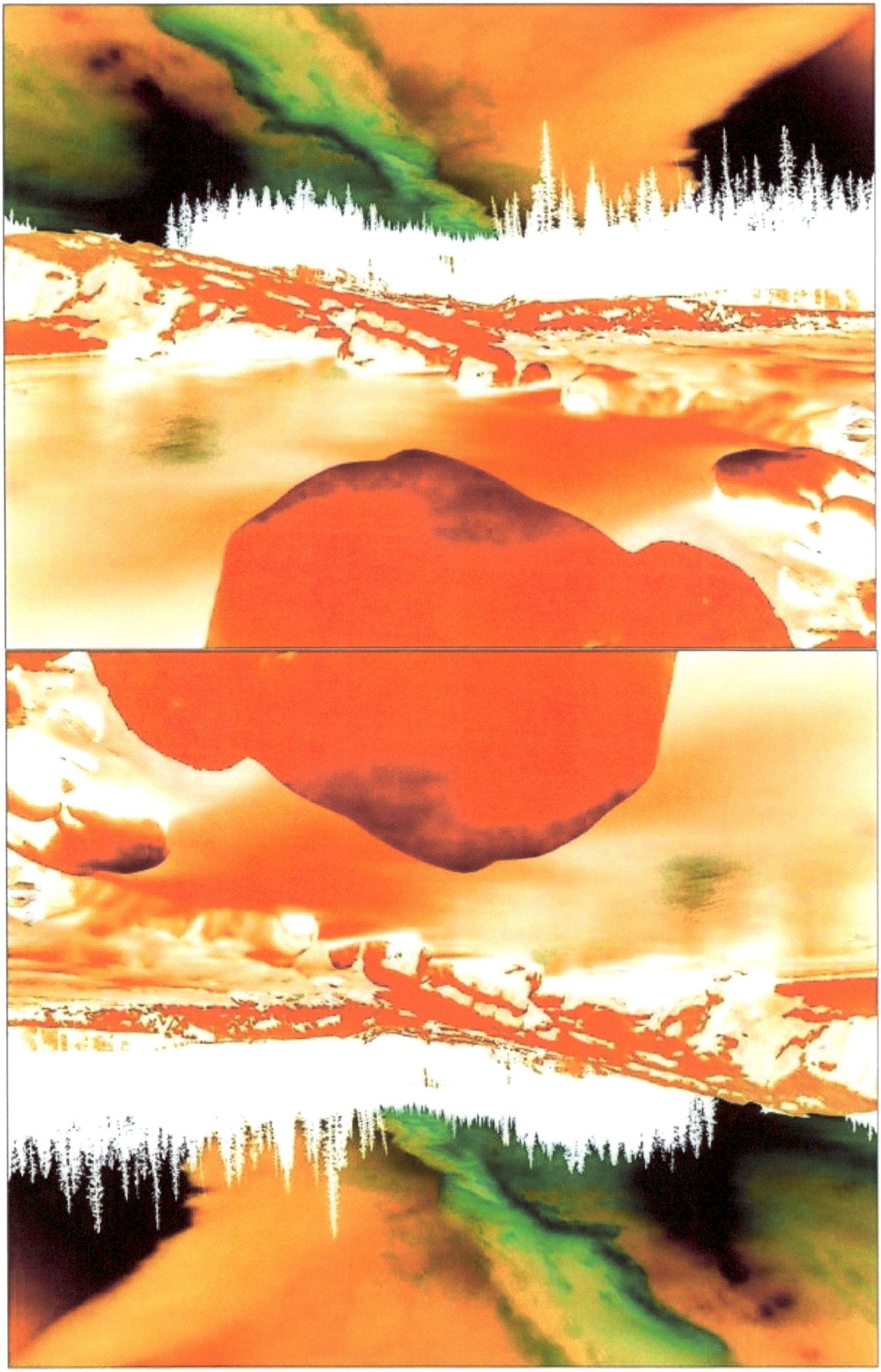

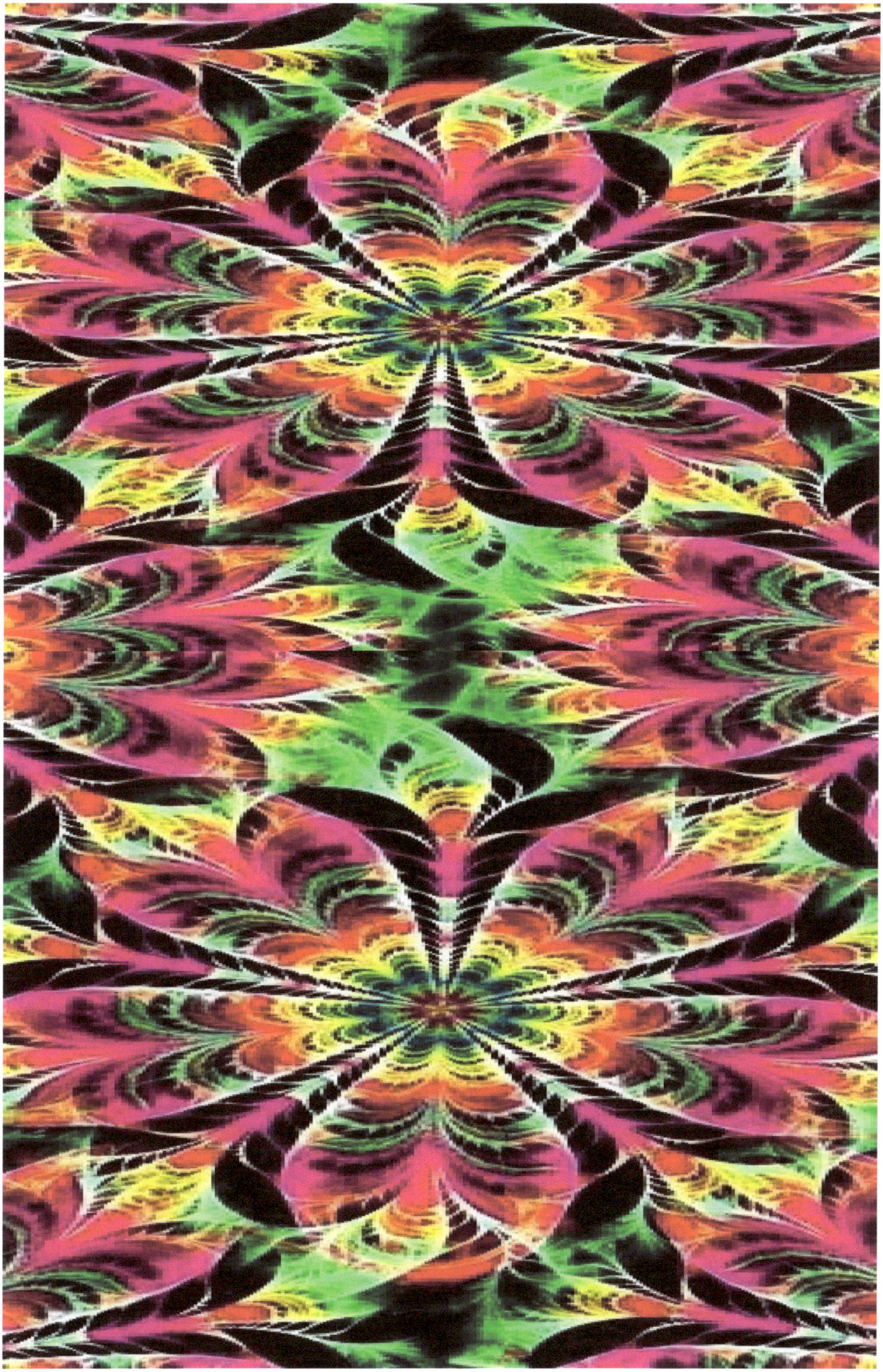

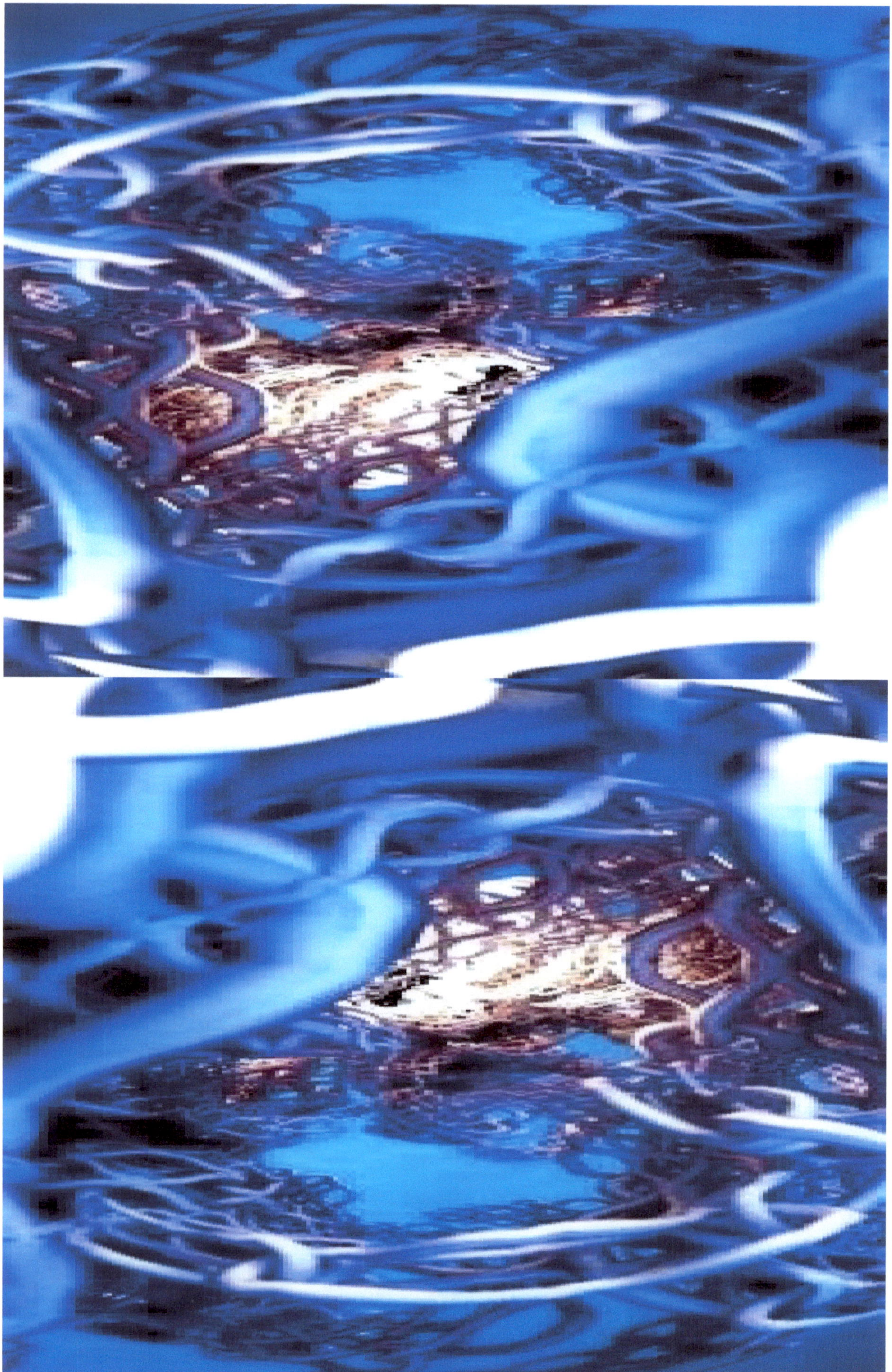

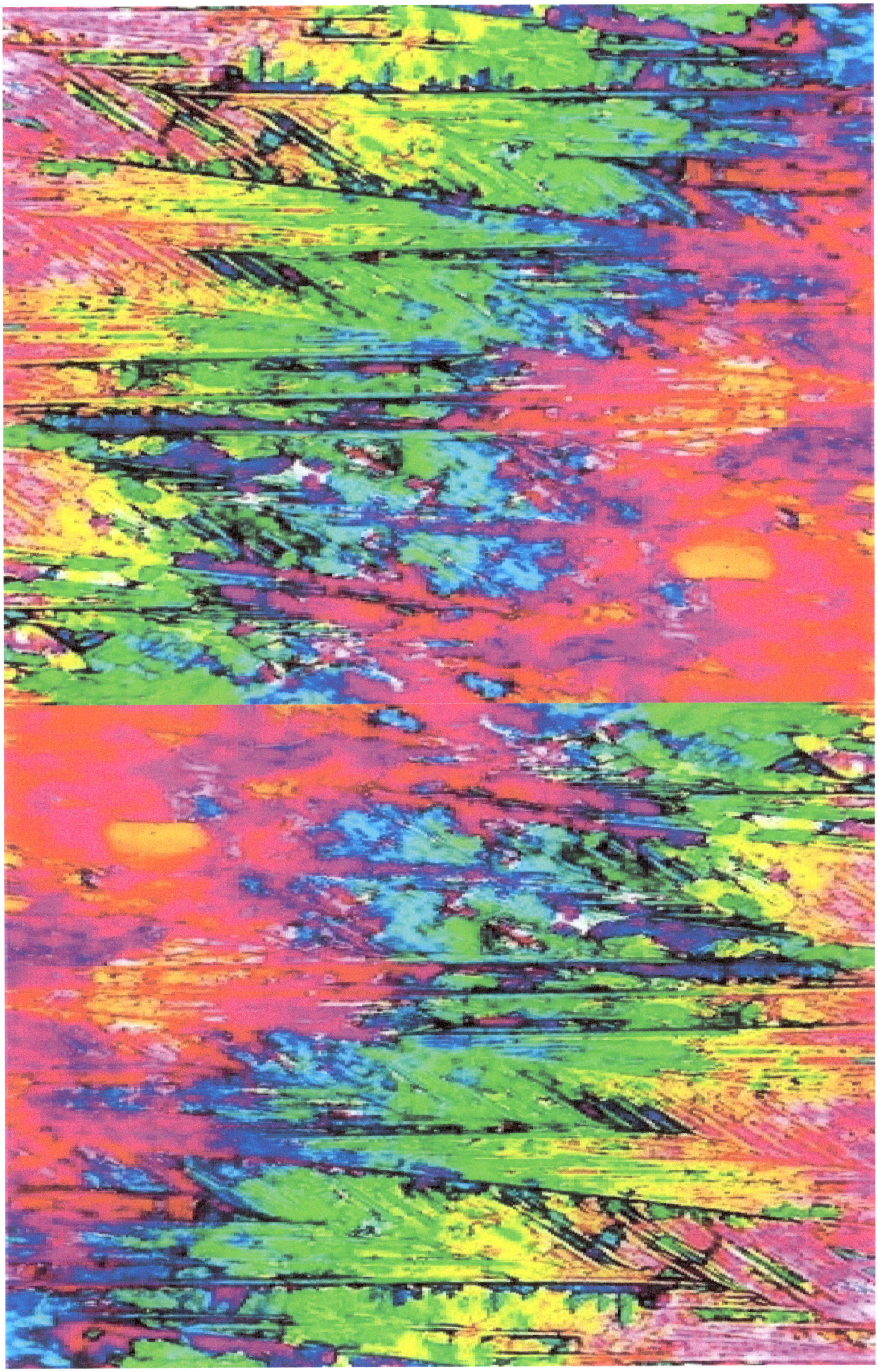

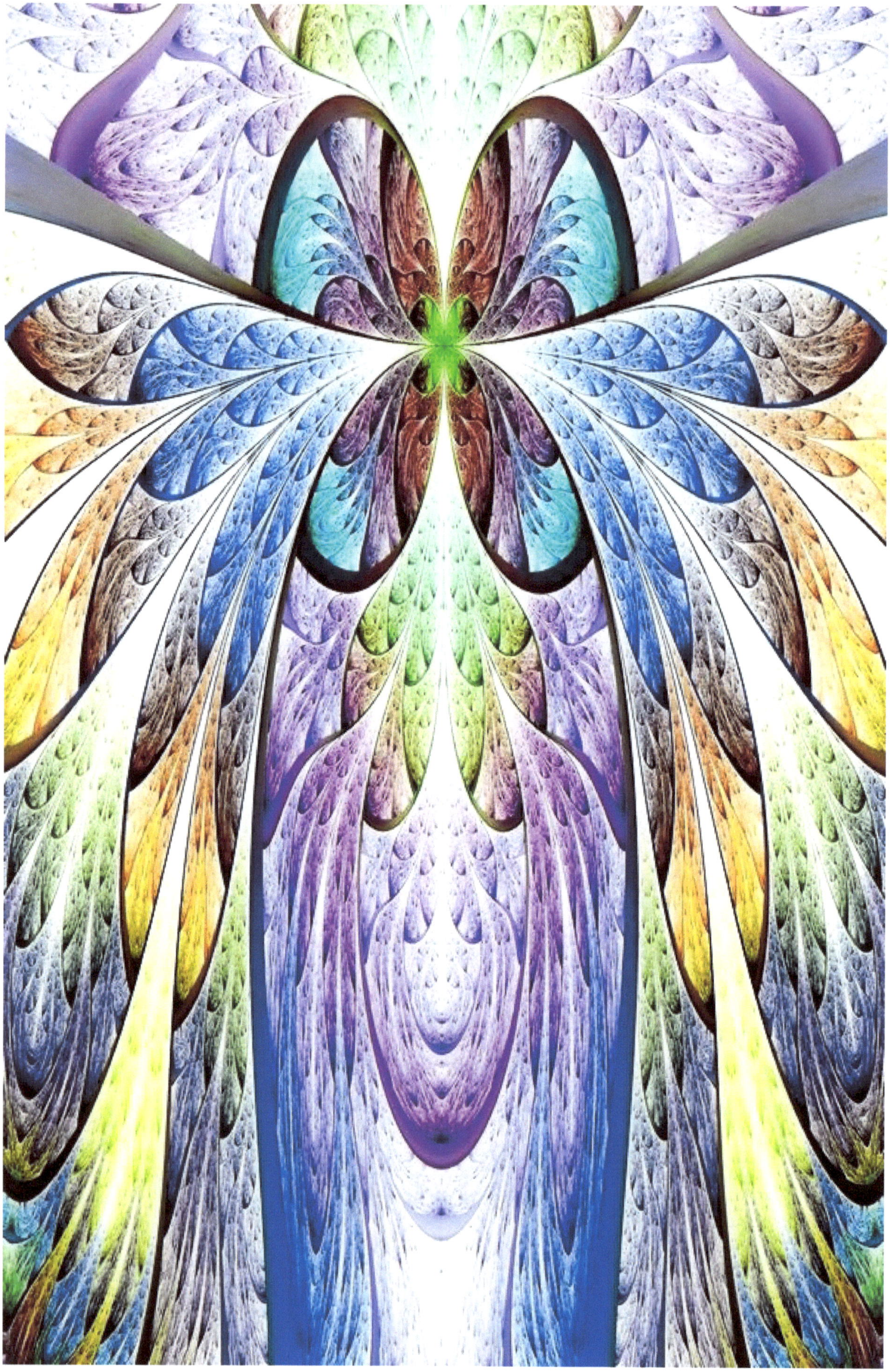

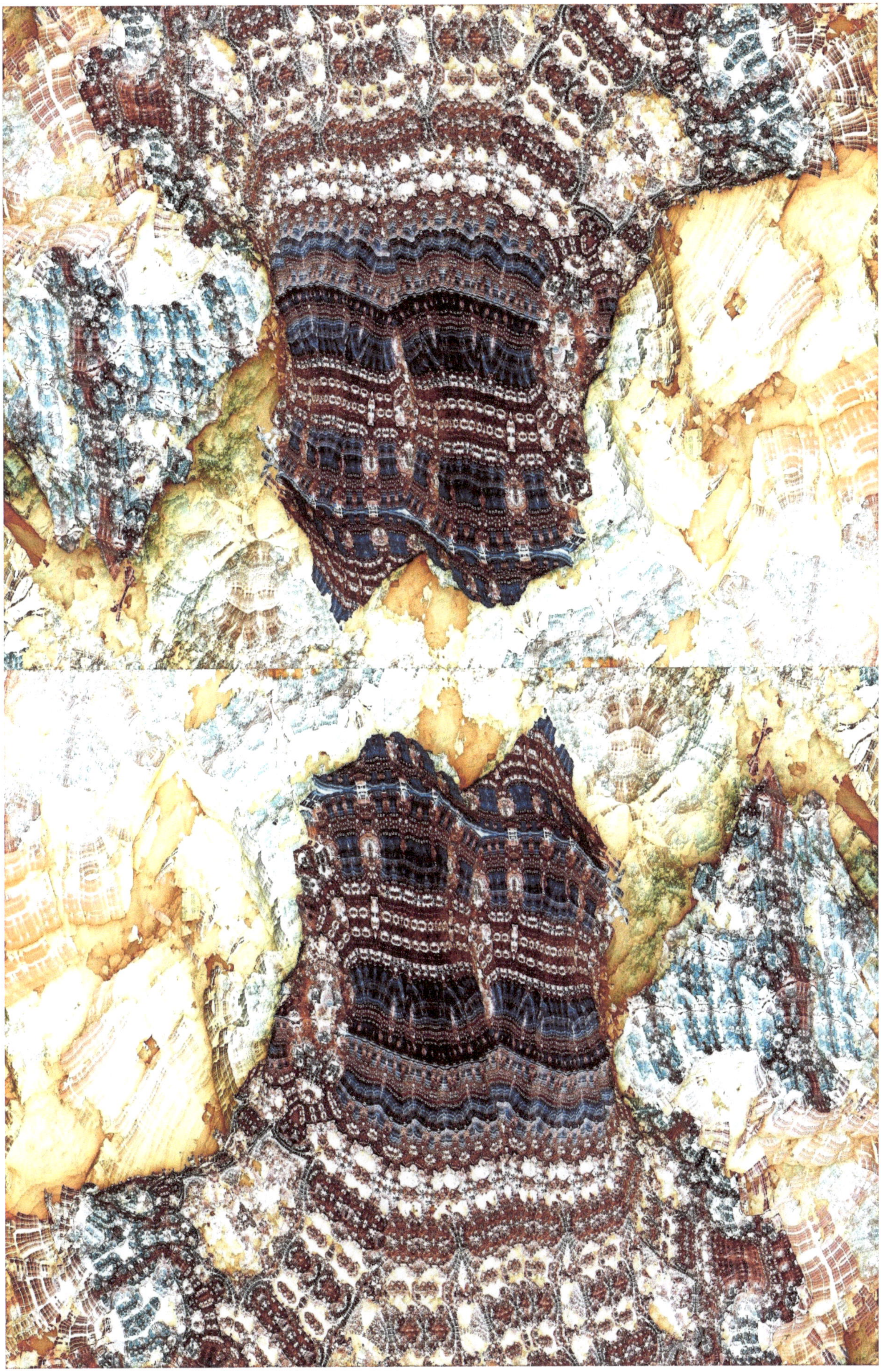

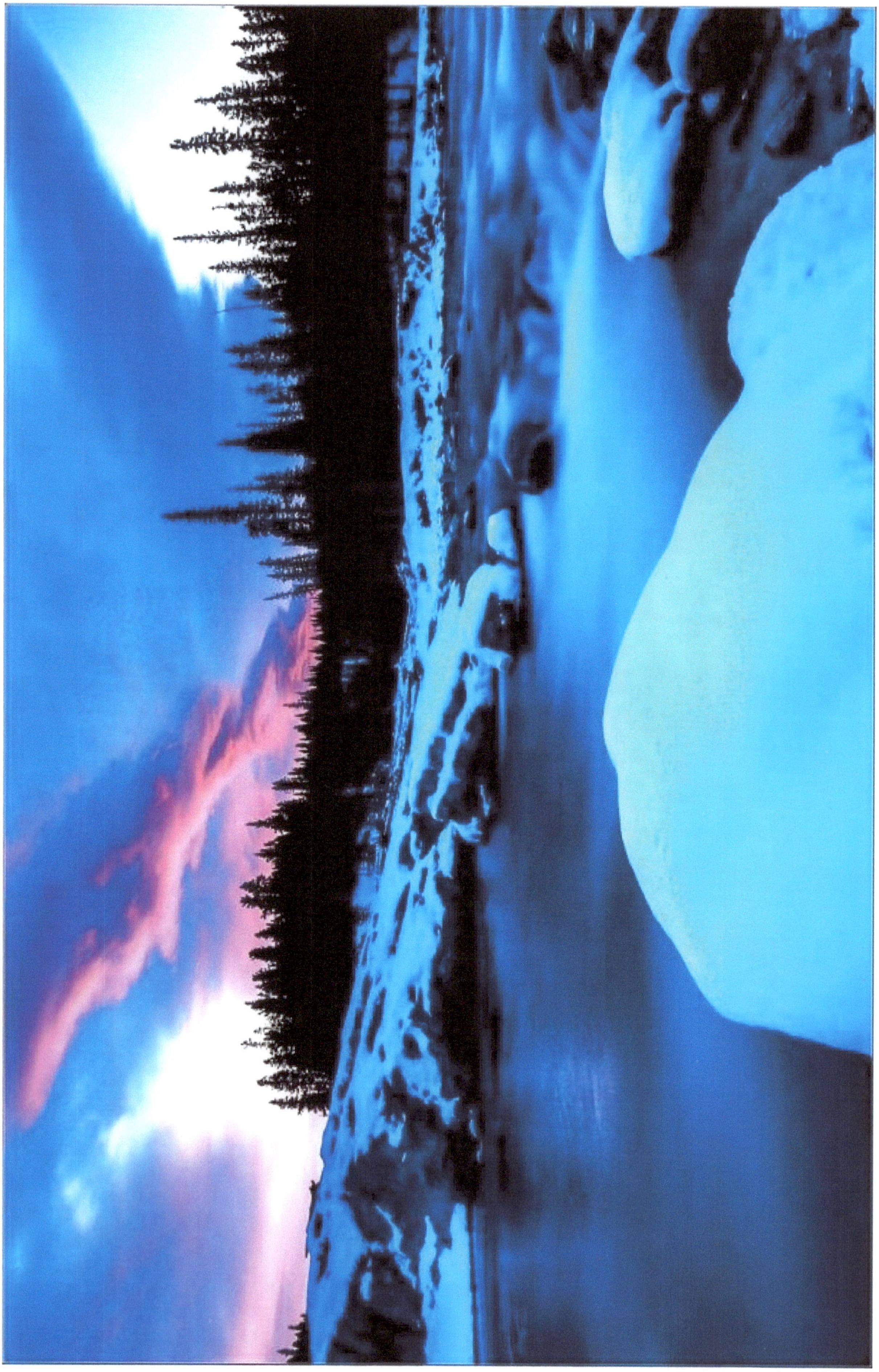

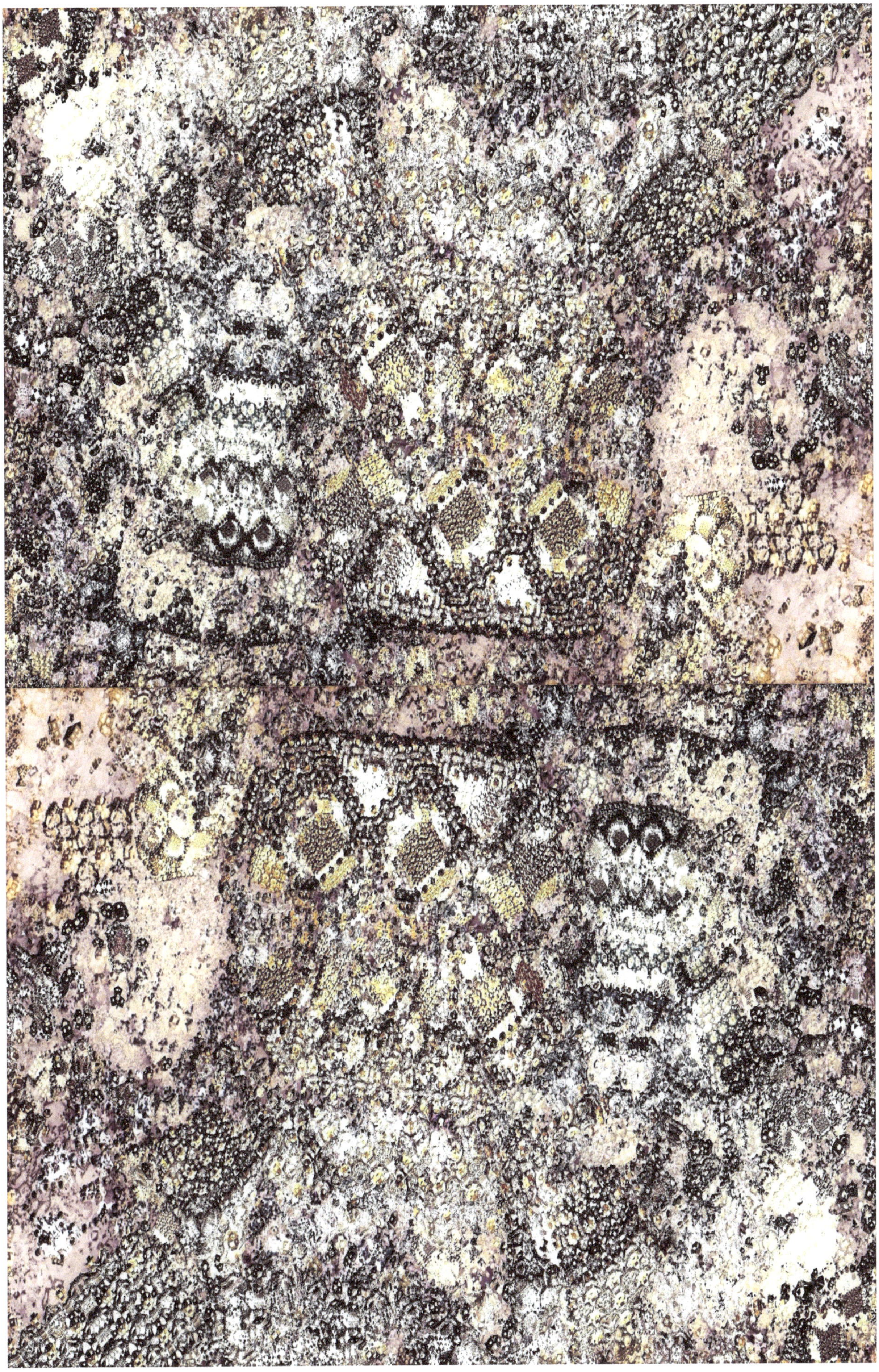

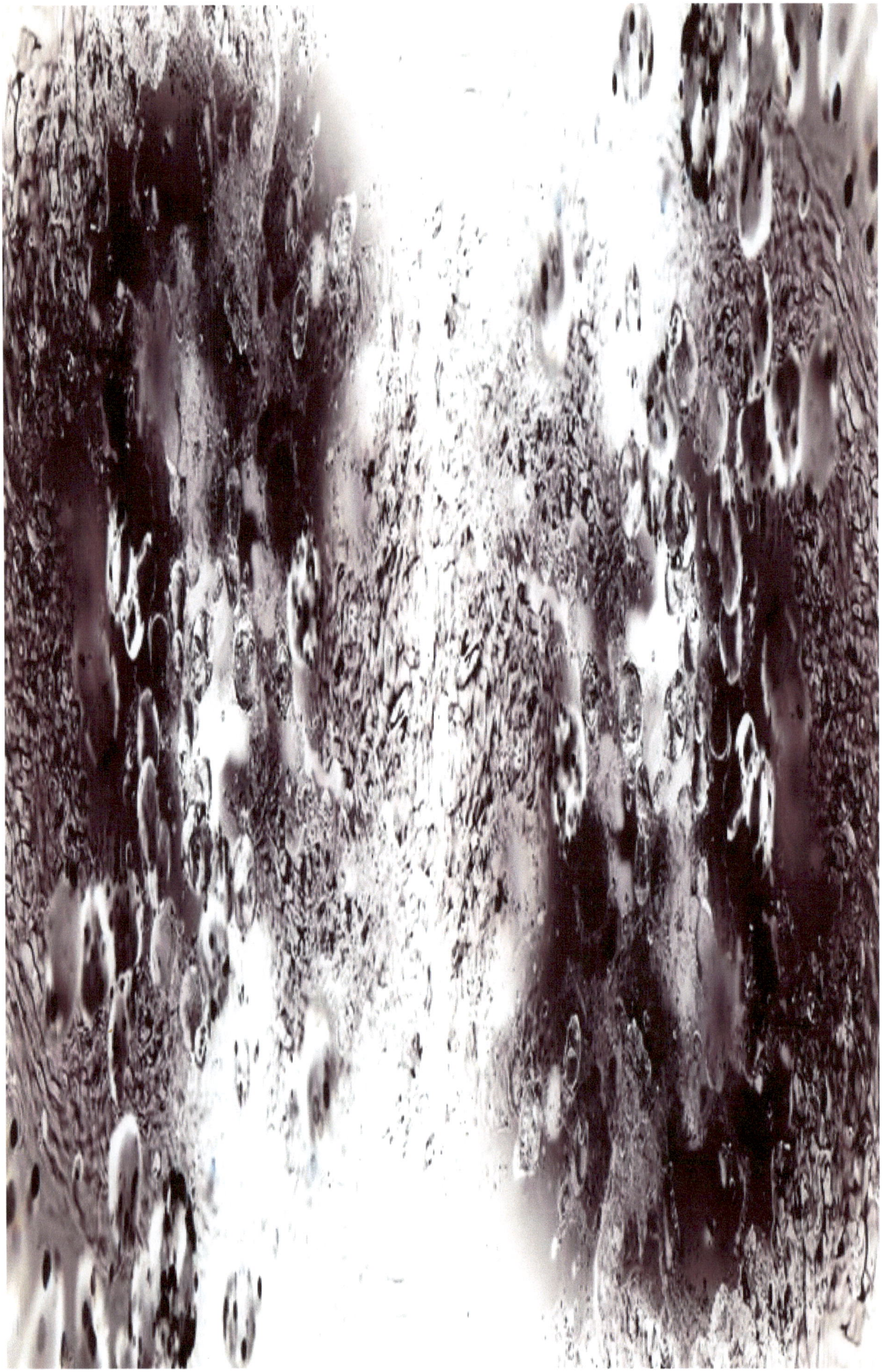

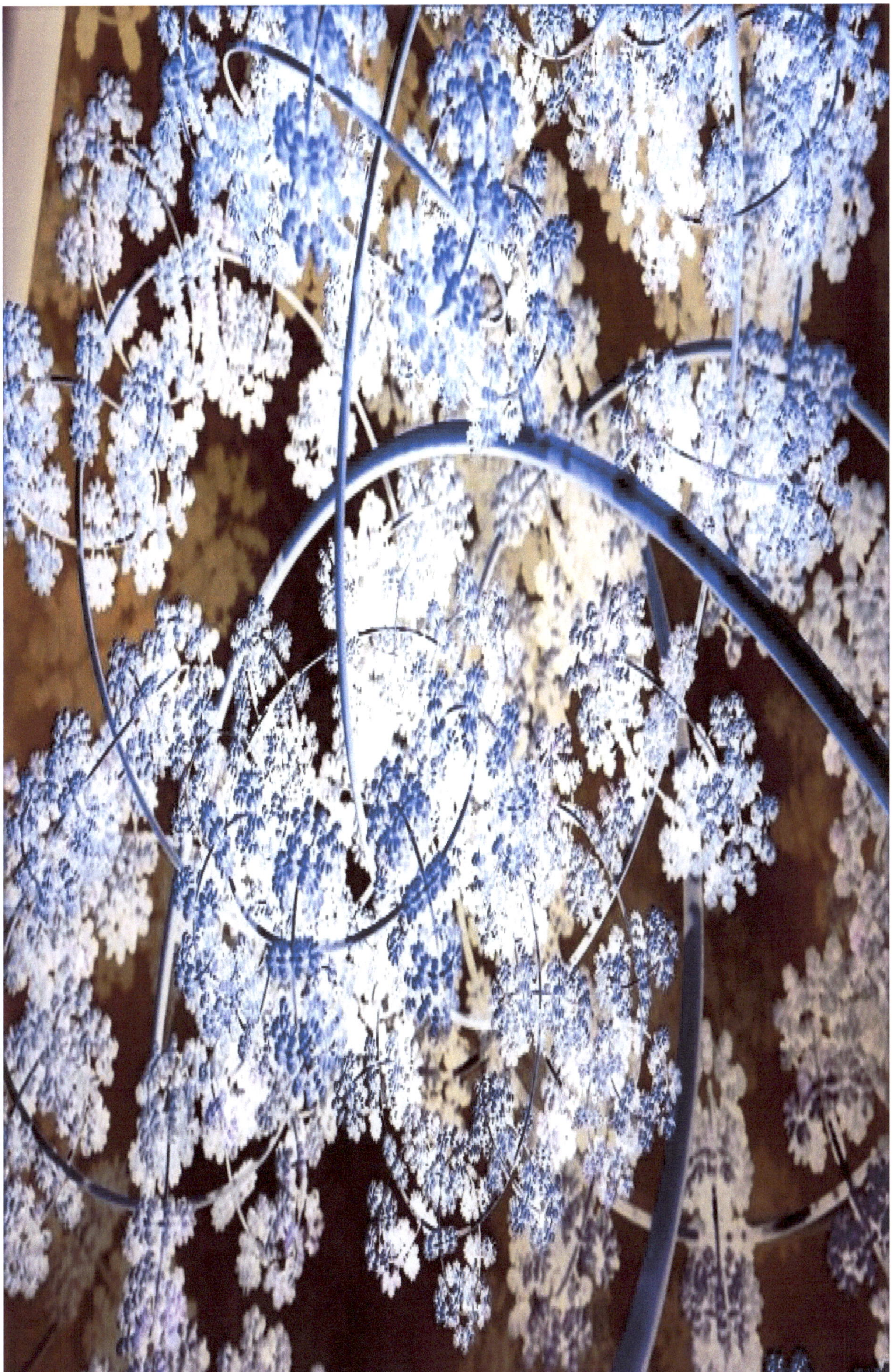

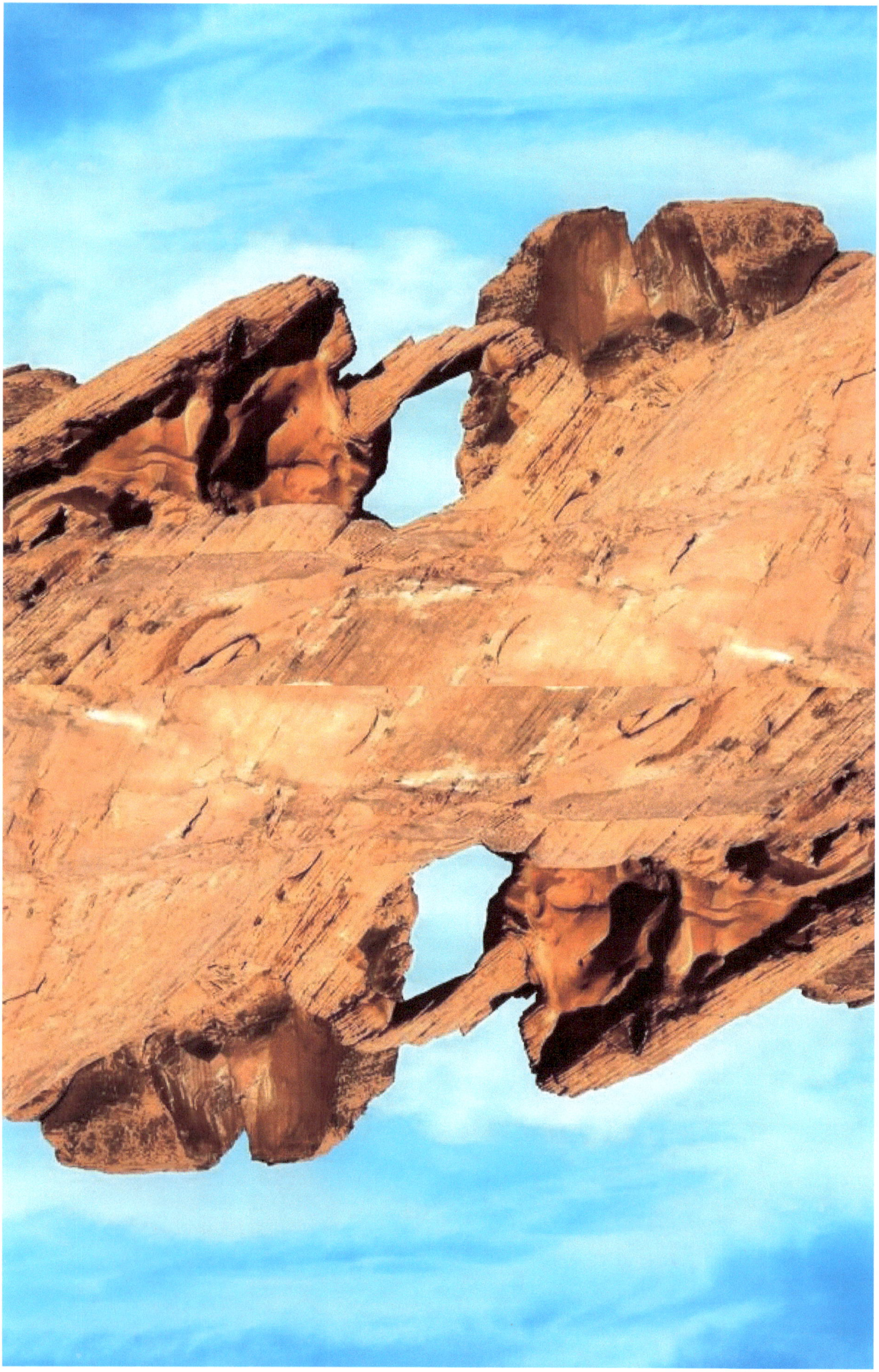

Mysterious Arya Bàhram

www.ingramcontent.com/pod-product-compliance
Lightning Source LLC
Chambersburg PA
CBHW051216220526
45473CB00003B/1051
* 9 7 8 1 7 1 8 7 1 9 7 1 2 *